THE DREADED RESEARCH PAPER

ALSO BY LARRY PATRIQUIN

Inventing Tax Rage: Misinformation in the National Post

Agrarian Capitalism and Poor Relief in England, 1500–1860: Rethinking the Origins of the Welfare State

Economic Equality and Direct Democracy in Ancient Athens

Permanent Citizens' Assemblies: A New Model for Public Deliberation

Democracy and Social Rights: A Path Toward Equality?

The Dreaded Research Paper

A Writing Guide for Busy Students

LARRY PATRIQUIN

© 2025 by Larry Patriquin

All rights reserved.
Published by Larry Patriquin
North Bay, Ontario, Canada
larrypatriquin.com

Names: Patriquin, Larry, author.
Title: The dreaded research paper : a writing guide
for busy students / Larry Patriquin.
Description: First edition. | North Bay, ON: Larry Patriquin, 2025 |
Includes bibliographical references.

ISBN: 978-1-0690019-0-0 (paperback)
ISBN: 978-1-0690019-1-7 (Kindle)

Subjects: LCSH:
English language—Rhetoric—Handbooks, manuals, etc.
Report writing—Handbooks, manuals, etc.
Academic writing—Handbooks, manuals, etc.

Subjects: BISAC:
LANGUAGE ARTS & DISCIPLINES / Writing / Academic & Scholarly
LANGUAGE ARTS & DISCIPLINES / Rhetoric
REFERENCE / Writing Skills

Cover design: Amanda Weiss
Interior design and typesetting: Amanda Weiss
Logo design: Amanda Weiss
Kindle formatting: Laura Jones-Rivera
Copyediting: Timothy Pearson

The paperback book has been composed in Minion,
Freight Text, and Avenir LT.

CONTENTS

1. What This Book Is About *1*

PART I. BEFORE YOU WRITE
2. Research *13*
3. Reading *24*
4. Plagiarism *30*
5. Format *38*

PART II. THE BIG PICTURE
6. Title and Subtitle *47*
7. The Introduction *55*
8. Argument *71*
9. The Conclusion *81*
10. Citations *84*

PART III. THE MECHANICS OF WRITING
11. Paragraphs and Sentences *95*
12. Punctuation *116*
13. Quotations *125*

14. Words to Watch *136*
15. Writing Dos and Don'ts *145*

PART IV. THE END

Appendix 1: Nonfiction Books to Inspire Your Writing *161*

Appendix 2: Some Advice for Instructors *168*

Bibliography *172*

About the Author *175*

1. What This Book Is About

I wish I had owned a copy of a book like this one when, many decades ago, I entered university as a first-generation student. I had performed exceedingly well in high school but then found my transition to postsecondary education quite daunting. I quickly discovered that the strategies I had relied on for success, such as memorization, were no longer useful. This marked the beginning of a painful year or two of self-learning, but I eventually figured out how to read critically and write academic papers that most instructors would characterize as "solid." By third year, my grades had improved to the point where I could think about applying to grad school. Looking back, I am sure that this transition would have been much easier if only I'd had, close at hand, the guidance that fills the pages of this book.

About a decade after graduating with a bachelor's degree, I went on to earn a PhD. I then taught for twenty-five years at a small, mainly undergraduate university in northern Ontario, Canada. Like me, most of my students were "first gen," struggling to settle into their new surroundings. To help them out, I designed assignments that asked each of them to make an *argument*, usually along a continuum from entirely in favour of some perspective to entirely against it. As I marked and graded their assignments, I took notes on the mistakes I encountered repeatedly, with the goal of providing collective feedback in the form of class handouts. For this book, my own experience as a student and the knowledge I gained as an instructor are supplemented with research on the topic of writing, the best of which you can find in the bibliography (see part IV).

Like many students, you probably dread having to write a research paper, an argumentative essay that defends a thesis, because you are not sure how to begin. A research paper must be a sophisticated work that makes effective use of the scholarly literature while demonstrating a thorough understanding of the topic under investigation, a work that is occasionally descriptive but primarily analytical, *explaining* some phenomenon or other. It is a challenge to complete one of these beasts, because you must take pieces of information from various sources and meld them together, synthesize them, into a coherent whole while saying something that is worth saying. You must engage in a public conversation, weaving the ideas of other people with your own thoughts while packaging it all in lucid prose. Thinking through an issue makes this type of writing process much more of a challenge than, say, drafting a letter to your grandmother or explaining "what I did on my summer vacation." It's also more difficult than other writing tasks you will frequently undertake, such as a post in a discussion forum, a summary of a journal article, or an email to an instructor. Composing a first-rate poem is the only type of writing I can think of that's more of a workout for your brain.

Research papers can also be onerous because you must write them over a short period, perhaps just a few weeks, while other pressing assignments are bearing down on you. Still, this is the hothouse within which your writing will improve. And you should accept now that this learning process will be a lifelong battle. There are no shortcuts to mastering a skill which involves expressing yourself in series after series of connected words. Just do the best you can. Not all papers can be exceptional. Not all sentences can be diamonds.

Writing, then, can make you miserable. But it can also serve as a source of delight for your mind. For that joy to come through, however, you need to feel comfortable approaching the task at hand. Once you have a grasp of the basics, you can focus on taking your writing to a higher level, where readers will be interested not just in what you have to say but in how you say it. You are transforming from someone who has been mostly a reporter or summarizer of other people's ideas into a postsecondary student who will become an independent thinker, at the same time that you are cultivating an authorial voice, a voice previously unheard by the world.

This book highlights the hundreds of mistakes you must avoid if you want to produce quality research papers. In your courses, you might be assigned a specific question or accorded great leeway on the topics you can choose from. You might be given the research materials (typically online) in the form of articles, case studies, and so on, or you may have to find these materials on your own. For any type of research assignment, this book will give you a foundation of information, crammed into a small space, on how to structure and complete competent works that should get your grades comfortably into the B range and perhaps see them rolling across the line into the A range. An "A" paper is a polished paper, thoroughly grounded in research with a convincing argument, well organized and beautifully written from beginning to end. An "A+" paper is almost publishable; the student who can write one of these should head straight into graduate studies after they finish their undergraduate degree.

Unfortunately, there isn't room here to tell you everything you need to know to become a writer of superb research papers. To go even further, to take your prose from readable to exquisite, review the works I recommend at the end of most of the chapters under "Further Reading." This will be necessary if you want the assessment of your papers to move from "solid" to "excellent." In short, unlike the authors of most writing guides aimed at students, I do not pretend to have all the answers. But I have a good idea where you can find them. My recommendations provide you with what is basically a program of self-study, carefully selected and curated from the more than one hundred books I read as part of my research for this project (only about one-third of which I considered sufficiently worthy to include in my bibliography).

While this book is aimed specifically at what you need to do to complete a research paper, much of my advice, for instance on how to write unified paragraphs and coherent sentences, can be employed in any type of assignment. This includes a journal or diary entry, an essay that reflects on experiential learning, a field report from a community placement, an interpretation of a poem or a novel, a critique of a film, a dialogue between two interlocutors, a case study of a business, a "one-minute paper" written in class, or a take-home exam. This is especially so because most of these assignments ask you to develop an argument in your head and then transfer it into an elegant stream of words.

In the last few years, though, some students have come to believe that because of the magic of artificial intelligence (AI), they should avoid exercising their minds while outsourcing the completion of their papers. This is a tragic mistake, however. For one, a work produced by AI is apt to read as if it were written by a machine—probably because it was. Furthermore, that machine will not always be accurate, it will employ a fair bit of guesswork, and its summaries and arguments will almost surely be pedestrian. AI has even been known to provide citations to "sources" that don't exist (that is, it just makes stuff up). And if many students in your class are making use of this machine, your paper will sound like dozens of others, something guaranteed to irritate your instructor (or, more likely, put them to sleep).

AI tools are bound to become more sophisticated, and in some cases rather swiftly, so if your instructor permits you to use them for a particular assignment, they have some benefits. For example, if you suffer from writer's block, AI can help you develop an outline, reminding you of some key issues you need to discuss, which you might otherwise overlook. Even in these instances, though, you need to be critical. Ask yourself: Will the paper produced from this outline be far too long or much too brief? Do the proposed headings come in the proper order or do I need to rearrange them? Are there sections I should cut, perhaps for lack of space? And does my research suggest some key topics that were missed by the AI-generated outline?

Still, you need to be aware that writing is mastered over a lifetime of practice. If you don't write first drafts, for example, then you won't learn how to think about, plan out, and structure your work. You will choose not to struggle. You will sell yourself short. Even worse, a machine will tell you what *it* thinks. Meanwhile, the world is waiting to hear what *you* think. It's in the process of facing and overcoming obstacles that you discern how to deal with complexity and how to weigh the strengths and weaknesses of the argument you are sketching out, how to generate the words that will help you express your thoughts—*your* thoughts!—ever so eloquently. You might be able to get AI to compose a paper for you, one that receives a passing grade or possibly a decent one. But from deep inside yourself, a disturbing question will soon rise to the surface: Is this my work, a product of my brain, my hands, my soul? You never want the answer to that question to be *no*. In sum, you have only four years of postsecondary education to learn how to write well and think critically. If all your work is just output disgorged from an AI database, you might get a degree, but how useful will that degree be? If you don't learn advanced reading and writing skills at university, I guarantee you will never find the time to do so over a career that will likely last for four decades (or more).

Finally, you should know that I will have little to say about grammar. In my view, there isn't much point in studying it unless you want to become a grammarian. For most of us, the rules of writing can be acquired through processes of assimilation, and these processes begin from the moment we are born. Think of the last time you saw a toddler reading a book on grammar. You never have? That's because no one has! And yet, these little humans catch on fairly quickly to the basic tenets of their language, such as the different verb tenses for past, present, and future. They flounder every once and awhile—and make some cute mistakes—but they have a strong understanding of the basics by the time they arrive at school. They then keep this method of assimilation going their entire lives. The best way to learn grammar and style, then, is to become a voracious reader and, especially if English is not your first language, a voracious listener (for listening, I recommend concentrating on "nonfiction": news, sports, documentaries, and podcasts). In short, you don't have to stuff the rules of grammar into your head. Instead, you need to absorb the sounds you hear when you are listening to a speaker or to the whispering voice that talks to you when you're reading. *There is simply no other way to become a refined and articulate writer.* You will supplement that learning when you write—or struggle to write. You will unconsciously imitate the styles of the authors you have read, which helps to facilitate the growth of your singular voice. And don't worry about imitating others. You can't write exactly like someone else because you are not someone else. You are, for better or for worse, uniquely you.

Thank you for picking up a copy of this book. I hope you find it helpful. And I hope you have as much fun reading it as I had writing it.

A BIT OF HOUSEKEEPING BEFORE WE BEGIN

1.1. The people who stand at the front of college and university classrooms hold various job titles, including professor, instructor, lecturer, teaching assistant, tutor, and seminar leader. In almost all postsecondary institutions, these individuals have some responsibility for grading papers and marking them (that is, providing comments and other feedback to each paper's author). In this book, I use the generic *instructor* to refer to all these people.

1.2. Your instructors may give you grading criteria for your courses or even for your whole program. This book can serve as an addendum to these criteria and help you satisfy them. If there is a conflict between the advice given in this book and the advice from your instructors, then the answer to the question of how to proceed is simple—follow your instructors.

1.3. Note that examples in this book are italicized to separate them from the text, which makes for ease of reading. As a result, words that would be italicized in your paper, such as book titles, appear here in normal ("roman") font and vice-versa. So, an example in this book will look like the following:

This argument was developed by Sigmund Freud in Civilization and Its Discontents.

If you wrote this sentence in a paper, it would look like this:

This argument was developed by Sigmund Freud in *Civilization and Its Discontents*.

1.4. In some of my examples, I will, rather arbitrarily, employ Chicago, MLA, or APA citation styles. These styles will be covered in chapter 10 ("Citations").

1.5. I am not an "influencer" and I am not involved in "affiliate marketing." I receive no income should you purchase any of the texts I recommend under the Further Reading headings. My recommendations are based solely on the quality of the works.

1.6. Throughout my writing career, I have likely (inadvertently) broken many of the rules I recommend here—and you might find some instances of my carelessness in this book. I've tried to learn from my students' mistakes as well as my own. In my defence, I will give you the same advice I give to myself: Do your best.

FURTHER READING

You should purchase the following reference books. They are perfectly sized for students (and I dare say most faculty); they are neither bulky tomes nor thin, condensed works. They also have pleasing layouts with font styles that are easy on the eyes. For a dictionary, go with the *Paperback Oxford English Dictionary* (864 pages). For a thesaurus, note that there are a large number of them on the market, including many that use the *Roget's* name, so be careful to buy the one I recommend: *The New American Roget's College Thesaurus in Dictionary Form* (902 pages). Get the third edition published in 2002 (with the red cover). You might want to supplement the *Oxford* and *Roget's* volumes with *The American Heritage Desk Dictionary and Thesaurus* (847 pages), a two-in-one volume that has "dictionary entries with corresponding thesaurus entries on every page." You should also consult *Bryson's Dictionary for Writers and Editors* (398 pages), by Bill Bryson. It presents, in alphabetical order, commonly misused cases of "spelling, capitalization, plurals, hyphens, abbreviations, and foreign names and phrases."

For grammar, check the first half or so of chapter 5 ("Grammar and Usage," by Bryan A. Garner) in *The Chicago Manual of Style*, pp. 233–318, where he surveys nouns, pronouns, adjectives, verbs, adverbs, prepositions, conjunctions, interjections, and syntax. Beyond that, I have not perused the thousands of grammar books available, so I can't say which is best, but if you want one that's a bit more basic than Garner's survey (and you probably do), I suggest Grant Barrett's *Perfect English Grammar*. It is small and well-organized with an appealing design. If, like me, you get flummoxed by non-intuitive grammar terms and need help understanding them, then his book is likely as good as it gets. For a kinder and gentler introduction, see Patricia T. O'Conner's *Woe Is I*. It is an informative and entertaining guide through the minefields of grammar, with chapter titles such as "Yours Truly: The Possessives and the Possessed" and "The Living Dead: Let Bygone Rules Be Gone."

The book you are now reading covers what you need to know to write a brief, undergraduate research paper. For information that will help you structure and compose larger works, see my chapter "How to Complete a Doctoral Dissertation in This Lifetime: Some Marbles of Wisdom," a typescript of which can be found at https://www.researchgate.net/profile/Larry-Patriquin. While that chapter is aimed at students working on a PhD, its advice should also prove helpful to those writing a master's thesis (or major research paper) or even a fourth-year honours essay.

Finally, I'd like to give a shout out to Helen Sword's *Stylish Academic Writing*. Its target readership is the professoriate, yet every academic writer, including students, will find her suggestions helpful. I concur with her conclusion that "there is a massive gap between what most readers consider to be good writing and what academics typically produce and publish." Sword's book is rooted in the belief that "elegant ideas deserve elegant expression," and she provides many pointers on how to approach this ideal.

PART I. *Before You Write*

2. Research

During the quarter-century that I taught postsecondary students, almost all the papers I gave low grades to suffered from the same problem, which was *not enough research*. Those who earned high grades understood that comprehensive reading always produces more sophisticated papers. Without detailed research, your argument will be overly general and repetitive. It will be obvious that you are filling space with banal observations. You will run out of topics to discuss. You will be a well with no water.

As a result, you must do more than skim a handful of pages in a couple of less-than-stellar sources. Knowing this, then, you should always undertake a significant amount of research, as much as time permits. You will make use of secondary sources (which I focus on), such as books and articles containing analyses of issues, written by scholars, practitioners, journalists, essayists, memoirists, poets, and the like. In addition, if you are in a discipline like history or anthropology, you will use some primary source research materials, which you will be expected to summarize and interpret, such as government documents, art objects, photographs, interviews, diaries, letters, novels, and surveys.

You must comprehensively read and understand your research texts. You then use these texts to shape your argument, whatever your argument may be. You extract the most important information from your sources, then elaborate on what you find while integrating it into an intelligible analysis. Your paper extends in imaginative ways the materials you gather during the research process, synthesizing the ideas of other writers with your own. You begin with a thesis (say, "Reversing declines in fertility rates will require the abolition of patriarchy"). You then defend that thesis by incorporating theoretical insights and evidence from the best of what you read. When you are done and a reader checks your sources, they should typically see you moving around somewhat from one to another.

In order to formulate strong arguments, you have to draw on scholarly materials. This mostly means books, chapters in edited books ("edited collections"), and articles published in academic journals. You can also use "popular" sources such as magazines, newspapers, and information found on websites, but use these more as supplementary materials. Do not rely on them exclusively as a way to avoid more challenging works.

So, how do you locate appropriate sources? To find books, you need to search your library's online catalogue. In North America, the subject headings you will come across have been created by the Library of Congress in the United States. The catalogue helps you decide which terms to use. For instance, if you enter *social welfare* in the subject line, you will receive thousands of results. This is far too many, so in this case the system will graciously offer you more than three dozen precise options, including *charities, endowments, human rights, human services, humanitarianism, international relief, philanthropy, public welfare, social problems, voluntarism, war relief*—and even *celebrities*.

You will need to experiment somewhat to settle on the terms most useful for your search. For example, if you type in *eating disorders*, you will find some books. In addition, you will be advised to check, among others, *anorexia nervosa*, *body image*, *bulimia*, *compulsive eating*, and *eating disorders in literature*. (If you are getting stuck at this point, don't be afraid to ask a librarian for help; that's why they exist.) Once your search has produced a number of results, you can check the individual records, the books themselves. You need to copy out or download the information, such as author and title, but especially the *call number* (for example, HV249.E89 P38 2007), unless it is an ebook, which of course you have immediate access to onscreen.

If your library does not have a specific book (or article) that you need, you can usually obtain it through interlibrary loans. Limit these loans to materials that are essential for your assignment, for which you can find no suitable substitute. This is something you would typically do only for a more consequential project, such as a fourth-year honours essay. Place any orders long before your due date because it may take a few weeks for these loans to be processed.

Articles are your other main research source. They are published in periodicals, which appear on a regular basis, usually monthly, quarterly, semi-annually, or annually. The most relevant periodicals come in the form of academic journals and magazines. A journal contains articles written by specialists in a field of study. These individuals are typically university professors or practitioners (social workers, psychologists, medical doctors, and so forth) who report on their own research findings. You can spot journals by their titles. They tend to contain words such as *Annals*, *Annual*, *Bulletin*, *Quarterly*, *Policy*, *Proceedings*, *Research*, *Review*, *Society*, *Studies*, *Theory* and, no surprise, *Journal*. Many others are exact descriptions of the research topic under review, including *Church History*, *Critical Care Nurse*, *Ecology*, *Eighteenth-Century Studies*, *Evolution and Human Behavior*, *Mathematical Programming*, *Teaching Philosophy*, and *Urban Geography*. This aspect of scholarship is a cornucopia; there is an academic journal for almost every topic imaginable.

Journal articles can be found in comprehensive indexes, which include, but are by no means limited to, Academic Search Premier, Education Resources Information Center (ERIC), Historical Abstracts, Humanities International Index, JSTOR (Journal Storage), MathSciNet, Nursing and Allied Health, Philosopher's Index, PsycINFO, Scholars Portal Journals, and Sociological Abstracts. You need to consult at least one of these indexes if you want to undertake a thorough search of what is available.

You can check through individual indexes, though most libraries now have "federated searching," which makes it possible to pull together information from various databases. I conducted one of these "macro" searches in my university library catalogue by typing the words *poverty and hunger* in the subject line. Employing other search modifiers, I asked for only journal articles published in English between 2014 and 2024. I had 1,049 results. Using the sidebar under *subject*, I was given the option to narrow this large list to *children* (129 results), *developing countries* (133), and *malnutrition* (145), among a dozen or so others. I could narrow these results even further by choosing particular databases, such as Sociological Abstracts, or journals, such as *American Journal of Public Health*.

Google Scholar is another type of "macro" index you can use as part of your research process. It will give you quick access to articles (and books), usually arranged in order; those at the top of every search result are those most cited by other scholars. A portion of the articles in your search may come as PDFs, which you can immediately download. You can also limit your search to a specific period (say, 2020 to the current year) if you want to focus on the latest publications. I use Google Scholar frequently, as it does have its virtues. For instance, it includes book chapters (in edited collections) which are sometimes overlooked by indexes. Still, indexes are necessary for comprehensiveness. And you can also guarantee that articles in academic databases are the final, published versions and not, say, the working papers or conference presentations you might get with Google Scholar.

When you have some sources at hand, take a look at their notes and/or bibliographies (or works cited or references lists). If you see a source repeatedly cited by others, check it out; it will likely be useful. It is an immense contribution to scholarship when authors bring works to our attention that we are not familiar with, that strike us as important, perhaps even fascinating, ones that we need to get our hands on immediately.

You now know how to find articles (as well as books). Your next step is to develop a research strategy. You have to draw the line somewhere, but you should feel comfortable that you know what is available and that you have checked the most important indexes. If you are looking for specific information, you should start with specific indexes, then broaden your search if necessary. Some researchers move from the general to the specific, yet they would get more precise results by proceeding in the opposite direction. For example, if you are writing on a topic in the field of education, the first index you should consult is ERIC (Education Resources Information Center). If you take this approach, the odds are you will quickly locate far more articles than you can hope to read in the time before your paper is due. If this happens, you might want to narrow your topic (in consultation with your instructor), so it can be addressed adequately in the allotted space.

Once you have your collection of journal articles, you have to read them. They certainly are more challenging than magazine articles, but with persistence you will eventually become more comfortable with their various styles of argumentation and presentation. It is also true that some journal articles are dreadfully boring, replete with unstylish writing, so if you have perused the abstract, scanned the text, and read a few pages, and it seems dull or uninformative, don't hesitate to dispense with it (unless it's a classic). There are likely countless more articles in the database you can use instead.

You may also incorporate magazine articles into your research, though note that while they cover issues like science and public policy, they are generally written by journalists who have not conducted the research themselves. These writers are summarizing the ideas of scholars, with the goal of reaching a broad audience. For the most part, avoid magazines (except, say, if you are studying how the media cover a certain subject). Magazine articles are easy to read—and they may be accompanied by a few pretty pictures—but you will have to use journal articles if you want to add depth to your research. One exception to this rule is magazines whose contributors are academics, practitioners, and/or highly respected journalists. They often write for publications such as *The American Prospect, Anthropology Today, Hammer and Hope, Harvard Business Review, History Today, n+1, The Nation, Red Pepper*—and hundreds of others. They are well worth consulting.

Perhaps the most important discerning feature of quality research sources is the practice of peer review, whereby manuscripts are assessed by other scholars in the field prior to publication. Having sources that always use this type of review is essential if you are a student in article-based disciplines such as psychology, mathematics, and chemistry. In other disciplines, there is a bit more leeway in incorporating non-peer reviewed work into your research. There are plenty of smart people in the world who are not academics. There are also plenty of smart academics who publish "trade" books, meant for audiences that are not exclusively academic. In these cases, manuscripts are typically vetted by a publisher's editorial board, as opposed to peer reviewed by scholars. These works are produced by companies such as Knopf, Norton, Penguin, Random House, Simon & Schuster, and (my personal favourite) Farrar, Straus and Giroux. Academics who publish with these presses are often the leading lights in their fields, so pay attention to them.

In the course of evaluating sources, I'd say the main questions you need to ask are: *Who is this author? Where did they earn their university degrees and what was the subject matter of those degrees?* Visit their personal website (which might be their own or one linked to their home university) and read their curriculum vitae (CV) or a list of their published works. If they are an academic, you still wouldn't want to give too much credence to one, say, with a PhD in English literature who is writing on astronomy or one with a PhD in astronomy who is writing on English literature. Experts need to write in their areas of expertise, which is why you will not hear a peep from me on how to judge the various translations of Homer's *Odyssey* or the best way to clone roses. So someone with a PhD in, say, economics should be ignored if they are telling us they have discovered that the measles vaccine is ineffective and can cause autism. If in assessing an author, you sense that something is "off," that they seem slightly deranged, then they probably are. Give them a wide berth. Research sources are an endless buffet. Keep pushing your tray down the line until you find the choicest cuts.

Another question to ask is, *Who is the publisher?* Check their history on Wikipedia for background information then visit their website—its aesthetic quality alone ("The year 1998 called; it wants its website back") can tell you much that you need to know, though not everything. There are many small presses that have excellent reputations, but work on tight budgets; they may not have the jazziest of websites and may even be soliciting donations to keep the lights on. If a publisher is disreputable, though, it's likely to be quite small. Oftentimes, it's obvious which ones are good and which ones are bad, but there are some "predatory" journals, for instance, that have the trappings of traditional scholarship (an editorial board, a submissions process, volume and issue numbers, and so on). They are set up by companies to earn money, requiring fees from prospective authors, many of whom are not qualified academics, in return for "publication" (see https://beallslist.net).

Separating the good from the bad is even more difficult when we leave academia and step into the hydra that is the worldwide web. You will find there plenty of legitimate academic organizations and research centres. But you will also encounter conspiracy theorists, corporate public relations hacks, social media sites owned by billionaires, "think tanks" funded by wealthy donors whose "findings" always (coincidentally?) match the desired outcomes of those same donors, and "astroturf" (as opposed to grassroots) organizations, supposedly representing ordinary people but—again—funded by the well-heeled. Once you move beyond standard academic sources, namely books and journal articles, you will have to be wary of the many traps set for the gullible that uncritical readers can fall into.

Overall, then, an academic who is writing on subject X should have a PhD in X (or a close disciplinary relative of X) and their work should appear with a reputable publisher. Even once these criteria have been established, however, you are not required to agree with everything a person has written. You have merely separated legitimate sources from illegitimate ones. Your next task, a more demanding one, is to work through the legitimate sources and discern strong arguments from weak ones. So for example, if our academic with the PhD in economics wants to try to explain to you the relationship between minimum wages and unemployment, you should give them a hearing. But their PhD and their 68-page CV, overflowing with peer-reviewed articles in top-tier journals, does not make them immune to criticism. You should be impressed by this individual's credentials and their scholarly accomplishments, but you don't need to bow down before them. That's the beauty of intellectual life—the endless back and forth, the endless struggle as we all grope our way to some "truth" or another.

As you conduct your research, you will discover that there are other sources available, aside from books, book chapters, and journal articles, but because of their limitations they should be used sparingly. They include:

(1) Encyclopedias (like *Encyclopedia Britannica*), which contain brief entries on a wide variety of topics. They are often great sources of factual information; for instance, if you want to know

the latest federal election results in Canada in every constituency, check out the article in *Wikipedia*, which is superbly organized and presented—so much so that it puts Elections Canada's cumbersome database to shame. In university, however, you should not use this type of encyclopedia in your formal assignments. You can, though, check publications that are better than the "high schoolish" encyclopedias, like *Britannica* and *Wikipedia*, because their entries are written and edited by specialists. These include (among hundreds or thousands of possibilities) *The Cambridge Encyclopedia of the Jesuits*, *Encyclopedia of Neuroscience*, *The Routledge Encyclopedia of Traditional Chinese Culture*, and the *SAGE Deaf Studies Encyclopedia*.

(2) Dictionaries, such as the *Funk and Wagnalls Standard Dictionary*, which give the meanings of terms. While they are useful for checking the spelling and generally agreed upon definitions of words, you should never use this type of dictionary in an academic paper unless you want to critique those definitions. Do not have a sentence in your paper that begins with something like, *According to the dictionary, "justice" means...*, with the implication that this definition is unproblematic. This is an especially egregious error if you are given a challenging article to read on the subject of justice, but you do not consult it. Also, just like the advanced encyclopedias, there are numerous advanced dictionaries, such as *The Cambridge Dictionary of Philosophy*, *The Concise Dictionary of Mathematics*, and *Historical Dictionary of Popular Music*, whose articles are written by experts. Feel free to consult them for your assignments.

(3) Newspapers (like *The New York Times* and *The Guardian*), which have their uses, for example as primary sources in higher-level historical research. But their articles, like those in most magazines, may prove to be less than enlightening. This is because journalism typically involves reporting on current issues, often under tight deadlines, rather than creating knowledge. While there are some informative columnists, most of what passes for

analysis in our daily newspapers is lacking in quality, and hence of little value for the types of assignments you will undertake in university. This is particularly the case if you are writing a paper that challenges the status quo or focuses on groups that are standing up to powerful interests. Again, you are permitted to use these sources but do so infrequently, perhaps to back up a single point or statement as part of a larger argument.

(4) Government documents, which are often meant for use by the general public and are easily accessible thanks to the web. Whatever the issue, chances are your government has commissioned a study on it. These are usually wonderful summaries of public policies, written by civil servants or outside experts, on just about any topic you can think of, and they should be consulted. At the same time, certain government publications (especially annual budgets and various "reports" sent to "taxpayers") are partisan, in some instances to the point of being quasi-propaganda. They often present the ruling political party's actions in the best possible light and so should be read with a critical eye.

(5) Websites, which contain vast amounts of information, often provided free of charge to users. The main problem with the web is a lack of organization and the growth of a whole mass of materials that are borderline junk (complete with graphic ads offering cures for foot fungus). Because of this, the web should be a supplement to your research rather than the first place you go, and it should never be the only place you go. The web is useful when you cannot find information from the best sources, namely books, book chapters, and journal articles. The web is especially good for lists of facts—such as the discography of just about any musical artist you can think of—but in academia we need to build our arguments on much more than bald facts (which, by definition, are uncontroversial).

And while it has its uses, the web does not make intellectual work easier. Do not go there looking for "the answer" to your assignment. If your instructor asks you, for instance, to read a difficult book, there's only one thing you can do. Bang your head against the book and read it. Especially avoid web encyclopedias. These sources are meant for students in high school (or even elementary school), and their articles should not appear in the bibliography of an assignment for a university course. If you use them, you will have the equivalent of a flashing neon sign in your paper that says, "I had no interest in doing the difficult work, the challenging work, my instructor asked me to do."

TIPS FOR RESEARCH

2.1. You need to undertake a comprehensive reading of relevant research materials. This will enable you to produce strong arguments. Note that limited engagement with research texts is often the major drawback of student papers.

2.2. Don't have a paper that is overly dependent on notes from class activities, such as lectures and videos. You need to use stronger, more sophisticated research sources.

2.3. Don't have a paper that is overly dependent on small sections from one or two research sources. This suggests you have not undertaken a detailed review of these sources.

FURTHER READING

The Craft of Research by Wayne C. Booth et al. is a classic text that has sold over one million copies. This very good book, with lots of tips for aspiring researchers, consists of five parts: Asking Questions, Seeking Answers; Sources and Resources; Making Your Argument; Delivering Your Argument; and Some Last Considerations.

3. Reading

This chapter provides some quick tips on how to engage in critical reading, which is the second task in preparing your paper, after you have gathered research materials. This task is not easy. Learning to read academic writing means you have to step up your game, the one that made you immensely successful in high school but which might prove less than adequate for university. In much of what you read, you will encounter dense prose and unfamiliar concepts, with arguments formulated by authors who assume you have more knowledge than you in fact do at this point. Despite this, you must push your way through. Don't get discouraged and give up. Do not hesitate to reread a text or at least the paragraphs you sense are critically important. Furthermore, when you are reading, do not run a highlighter lazily over the text, so that the page ends up looking like a banana peel. Any markings you make (and there shouldn't be many of these) should help you recall the thesis, the relationship between the various arguments, the supporting details, the views the author critiques, and your own questions for the author.

You must read academic works attentively, especially because there are different ways of interpreting any particular phenomenon. This can be frustrating at first. New university students typically want to know *the* answer, but often, especially in the humanities and the social sciences, there's not a single, definitive answer to most questions. For instance, how should we respond to the problem of unemployment? A conservative might argue for lower minimum wages, anti-union laws, and lower welfare rates. A Marxist might argue for the abolition of capitalism and an end to private ownership of the means of production.

Keep in mind, then, that every author has a point of view. Every author has a motive, an axe to grind, otherwise they would not bother entering debates. Most academics write when they are upset about something, or they see a "gap in the literature," an intellectual problem that needs to be addressed. So, you have to get used to the fact that almost every author is entangled in a controversy and is making an argument for one side of that controversy. Be aware that what is at stake rarely comes down to an either/or dichotomy. Usually, writers on both sides of an issue have many matters on which they agree, but other important ones on which they disagree. And this disagreement is not always obvious. Sometimes it seems as if an author is giving you nothing more than endless pages of description. This is especially the case in the textbooks assigned in many introductory courses. You scratch your head and wonder: "Is there an argument hidden in all this description?" The answer is *yes*. There is *always* an argument—though you might have to look closely to find it.

In addition to a unique viewpoint, every writer will make multiple "truth claims," claims that something or other is true, justified, preferred, fair, and so on. To be "critical" means to doubt these claims to truth. As a result, you must constantly *evaluate* what you are reading. To excel at this task, you need to *ruminate* (take in, chew over, let sit, re-chew as needed). Do not just absorb information the way a sponge absorbs water. You have to pick the text apart. Be aggressive. React, respond, disagree. *Oh, yeah? No way!*

Your job is to analyze and assess arguments, some of which you will reject as inadequate, as somehow lacking. Begin by discerning what the author is focusing on. What intellectual problem are they addressing? What is the writer's "take" or "angle" or interpretation of that problem? How do they propose to address it? And who are they arguing against, the people who may not even discern that there *is* a problem? When figuring this part out, do not make the common mistake of inattentive readers (or AI databases!) and attribute to the author something that they are in fact critiquing.

Your main task is to poke holes in every author's argument. A critical reader is a skeptical reader. Let's say an author claims that "Workfare in the United States has been an enormous success." Your first response might be: "*Enormous?* You're kidding, right?" (You can formulate a more professional response later.) Then ask: Is the author's argument convincing? What evidence is provided to support it? Has the author ignored crucial pieces of evidence that could challenge their assumptions or conclusions? Is the argument important, or is the author telling us something we already know? Have they merely "explained" the obvious?

Keep in mind, too, that a nonfiction author has to make many choices: what their thesis (argument) is and what evidence they will use to support it; how to narrow their topic; how to reduce the number of chapters (or sections) to a manageable size; plus the thousands of micro-decisions involved in structuring and writing a text. You get to see only the final product, with all the author's agony and teeth-grinding removed. Still, take care to note how an author might tell one aspect of a story but not another. For example, in a book on the history of the welfare state, they might pay much attention to class conflict while giving short shrift to race and gender, hence providing only a partial explanation of that history. Our author might say they left race and gender out of the picture for reasons of space. You, in turn, can reasonably respond that that's not acceptable, and that they needed to *make space* for these discussions. One of the toughest tasks of a critical reader, then, is to figure out *what is missing*. What did the author overlook? There probably won't be any factual errors in what you read; for instance, no one will claim that World War I started in 1904. What is "wrong" usually involves what is left unsaid, what the author did not consider.

Finally, note that most writers present a general argument then support it with specific details. As you attempt to discern this argument, pay attention to what the author is *doing*. Are they trying to explain, evaluate, define, classify, theorize—or something else? When reading, stay focused in particular on the opening paragraphs of a work, where the author should provide a thesis statement and a road map for the argument that is about to unfold. As you proceed, you will see that important ideas often appear in the first sentence of each paragraph (though not always). These are the "topic sentences." Sometimes the main idea is directly stated in these sentences, but sometimes it is not. When it's not, you'll need to search for it. In doing so, be careful you don't get sidetracked by all the details while missing the author's main point.

In this process of paying attention, keep an eye out for how an author uses transitions—when they signal that they are about to move from one paragraph to another, from one idea to another, where they might summarize what came before and indicate what is to come (*We have seen that…*; *We will now survey the three…*). Other transitions are more subtle and often take place within paragraphs. Watch for the following types of phrases (which you should incorporate into your own writing):

- those that show the relationship between ideas: such as *accordingly, at the other extreme, because, consequently, in contrast, in comparison, nevertheless, on the other hand, similarly, the result of all this…*

- those that point to the introduction of a new idea: such as *furthermore, in addition, let us now turn to, the purpose of this chapter, the second aspect of, there is another way of viewing*...

- those that take us from the main idea to the evidence: such as *for example, for instance, specifically, to illustrate*...

- those that conclude: such as *all in all, altogether, in brief, in conclusion, in sum, on the whole, to summarize*...

As you read for an argument, you will need to take notes, which like every skill employed in university is one that you may not have developed well during your time in high school, yet it's an important and often undervalued skill, which you should master. In the "real world" of work, you likely will be involved in numerous meetings, conferences, and presentations, which will require you to keep accurate and relevant notes for future reference. For the time being, taking good notes will prove invaluable as you prepare to write.

What you transcribe into your notebooks or electronic files will depend on how you learn. Some people prefer to process and synthesize information as they go, while others take what amounts to a verbatim copy of what they've read, leaving the synthesizing for later. Some like to conduct all their research before they begin writing, while others move frequently between a bit of research, then a bit of writing, drafting the paper as they go. I highly recommend this back-and-forth process, as it enables you to watch the paper rapidly forming, and you'll be able to prioritize what you need to read, from your large stack of research materials, to move it closer to the finish line. Ultimately, though, you have to discern what works best for you, as no two people have identical ways of turning reading and thinking into writing.

FURTHER READING

For a cogent survey of some of the key issues involved in academic reading while "entering into a discussion with the authors of your sources," see chapter 3 ("Interpretation: Reading and Taking Notes") in Gordon Taylor's *A Student's Writing Guide*, pp. 53–88.

See also Thomas C. Foster's *How to Read Nonfiction Like a Professor*. It's an engaging study of how to become a more effective reader. He is especially good on sources found in newspapers, on the web, and on social media, and his lessons are applicable to academic works as well.

4. Plagiarism

Plagiarism occurs when you fail to properly cite your sources. This means providing a note of some kind (an in-text reference, footnote, or endnote) which tells the reader that the information presented has been summarized, paraphrased, or quoted directly from a source such as a book, journal article, magazine article, blog, podcast, archival document, doctoral dissertation, personal interview, and so on.

At North American and British universities, among others, plagiarism is considered cheating, and students can be disciplined for it, receiving a grade of zero (or an "F") for an assignment or even for an entire course. If you are found to have plagiarized repeatedly, you may be suspended from university for a period (perhaps one academic year). In extreme cases, you may not be allowed to return. Ignorance of the rules concerning plagiarism will not be accepted as a defence. And note that you can easily be caught; all it takes is for an instructor to type a couple of your sentences into a search engine. Before you know it, you will be hauled before some ominously named academic committee where you, with tears in your eyes, will have to explain your misconduct.

Still, playing it safe isn't easy. Judgment must be used in discerning when to cite and when not to cite. The following are some general rules on how to proceed.

WHEN NOT TO CITE

4.1. When it is fairly obvious that all the material in a paragraph originates from a single source. In this case, you don't need to cite, say, three or four times, though you must have at least one citation, usually at the beginning or the ending of the paragraph.

4.2. When using facts that are "common knowledge." A rough test of common knowledge is: Would a TV game show host pose this question to a contestant? For example, "Who was elected prime minister of Canada in 1993?" or "Who won the Academy Award for Best Supporting Actor in 1953?" The answer to these questions would not require a citation.

Jean Chrétien was elected prime minister of Canada in 1993.

Frank Sinatra won the Academy Award for Best Supporting Actor in 1953.

4.3. When using facts that would lead most readers to say, "that sounds about right." These facts can be verified easily with a quick online search. For instance, *By early 2019, the national debt of the United States exceeded $22 trillion.* I have seen one student guide suggest that a fact like this one (they gave the example of the population of Beijing) would require a citation. In my view, this would clutter up your text with endless notes; though, as always, follow the guidelines from your instructors. Also, look closely at your course readings for their citation patterns and emulate them. They will range from the commonsensical patterns found in most disciplines to the citation of the information in virtually every sentence (for instance, in articles published in law journals).

4.4. When using a distinct phrase that at one time would have required a citation but is now considered a part of everyday speech. For example, *Almost everyone agrees that we are entitled to life, liberty, and the pursuit of happiness.*

WHEN TO CITE

Your paper should have approximately two to three citations per double-spaced page—that is, from twenty to thirty for a ten-page paper. If you have just three or four citations in a paper of this size, it suggests you are not giving sufficient credit to your sources (or you haven't used enough of them). More than thirty might constitute overkill. You do not require a citation for every sentence or every second sentence (unless you are in law school).

You must provide citations for the following:

4.5. Facts that are not a part of common knowledge and that cannot quickly be verified online. Do not quote this kind of information but do cite it.

Poor relief expenditures in Great Britain rose from £520,000 in 1751 to £4.2 million in 1803 (Smith 1968, 204).

4.6. Verbatim (word-for-word) quotations. Words taken verbatim *must* be put in quotation marks. Having only a citation without any quotation marks is *not* acceptable.

According to Ellen Meiksins Wood, the "idea of a peasant-citizen was even further removed from the experience of other ancient states."[4]

4.7. "Apt terms" and distinct phrases, ones you have not developed on your own. You are encouraged to learn new words and expand your vocabulary, but you must be careful when using another person's unique way of expressing themselves. So, in the following example, you would not want to try to claim the phrase "someone warm and breathing" as your own literary innovation.

Virginia Woolf notes that when we are writing a letter, we think about our correspondent; indeed, she maintains, that "without someone warm and breathing on the other side of the page, letters are worthless."[7]

4.8. When you paraphrase or summarize someone else's ideas, concepts, or interpretations. Some ideas, like the notion of the "invisible hand" of the market, are from a particular author (in this case, Adam Smith), but have been used so often they are now in the "public domain," part of ordinary language. Other ideas, however, are not in the public domain and so must be cited.

Gramsci's (1971, 59) notion of hegemony is helpful for...

This phenomenon is what Naomi Klein (2007) refers to as the "shock doctrine."

4.9. When you use someone else's approach to organizing ideas.

Johnston suggests that all revolutions go through three phases.[8] First,...

Ralph Miliband (1989, 19–55) argues for a four-fold division of social classes, including the dominant class (which itself incorporates a power elite), the lower middle class, the working class, and the "underclass."

The golden rule is: When in doubt, cite.

HOW TO AVOID PLAGIARISM

4.10. *Be careful when paraphrasing.* This is when you *restate a short passage* such as a paragraph in your own words. You especially must avoid what might be called the "too-close paraphrase," which involves taking sections of a text and substituting your own language every now and then for what's in the original. It usually entails rearranging sentences and cutting the odd word here and there while using a thesaurus to unearth synonyms that can serve as replacements for the authors' words. In these instances, your voice is weak throughout, while the reader can still hear a strong "echo" from the research materials. To stay out of trouble, combine paraphrasing and quoting by squeezing in a few short quotations from the author along with your own words. Having said that, the best way to avoid plagiarism is to avoid paraphrasing. When you try to convert a small section of a text—say, a sentence or two—into your own words, and you do this repeatedly throughout your paper, you greatly increase the odds of plagiarizing. Focus on summarizing instead.

4.11. *Learn how to summarize.* This is when you *condense an extended work*, such as a section of an article, an entire article, or a book. In a summary, you cut out most of the details. You can also integrate some quotations into your summaries, which would need to be cited.

4.12. *Learn how to quote.* You are permitted—even encouraged—to use insightful passages word-for-word as long as you put them in quotation marks (or have indented text blocks for long quotations) and identify your sources with citations. Keep in mind that if you string together a clothesline of properly cited quotations, you will avoid plagiarism charges, but you will also produce a less than worthwhile text, one containing almost no original thinking. Your own expressions must dominate the narrative. That's what you're aiming for. As you write, you must hear an intelligent conversant in your head, firm and forceful, the *you* who has something urgent to tell the world. Then you must transfer the insights you are channeling into a coherent text that you send to readers, a text that implicitly says, "Here's what I have discovered" (with the emphasis on "I").

4.13. *Take notes carefully.* Develop a method of recording your ideas that distinguishes the words and thoughts of the sources from your own. For instance, as part of your notetaking regime, put quotation marks around words taken verbatim from your sources. Equally important, always know where you obtained your material. Keep accurate bibliographic information, including page numbers, as you research and write.

4.14. *Conduct extensive research.* Students have a much greater chance of plagiarizing when they use only one or two sources and transfer ideas from those sources, in the same order as they were presented in the original, into their own papers. The probability of committing plagiarism increases even further if you read just a handful of pages from a few articles. If you do this, there's a danger that with constant paraphrasing, you will echo the author's voice, in a best-case scenario coming within a whisker of breaking the rules.

Conducting extensive research will help you avoid plagiarizing, and it will also enable you to avoid the "echo" problem. If you have a number of sources, you can integrate them into your paper in the way that you might, in a bowl, mix the ingredients for chocolate chip cookies. You combine distinct items (sugar, butter, chipits) to create something amazing, something genuinely yours. When it comes to writing, you will know you have succeeded in this process of integration when you start talking to yourself, when you begin to hear your thoughts, when you realize that you are contributing a new accent to the world of unique voices.

4.15. *Sketch out your argument.* This sketch can be in the form of a tree, one containing a number of branches that grow out from the trunk (which is where we would find your thesis). Set your research notes aside for a day or two, then using your "tree branches," begin writing the paper. Unless you have a photographic memory, this method will help you avoid repeating the phrasing of your sources. After you've written as much as you can, review your research notes and fill in the many gaps that will undoubtedly remain.

4.16. *Cite electronic documents.* Works found on the web are not floating in space, free for the taking. They must be cited like any other source, such as a book or a journal article. Also, if you plagiarize from the web, your nefarious act will be detected; all it takes is for your instructor to conduct a search in Google.

4.17. *Do not misuse artificial intelligence.* You should never use AI for any purpose unless you have been permitted to do so by an instructor. They might grant you a blanket permission for all assignments in their course or only for particular ones (and be sure to cite your AI sources). Without this permission, however, you must proceed on the assumption that when it comes to your assignments (be they papers, exams, thought journals, and so on), AI is off limits.

4.18. *Be careful with group discussions.* It is generally acceptable to get together with your fellow students to go over your assignments. Unless you are explicitly allowed to hand in the same work, though, you must write your own paper, featuring your own organization, your own writing style, and your own ideas.

4.19. *Don't self-plagiarize.* That is, don't hand in a paper, or even sections of one, that you wrote for another course. You may want to expand on a paper written elsewhere, and explore the issue in more detail, but if so, consult with your instructor first before undertaking the assignment.

FURTHER READING

You should own a copy of Gordon Harvey's *Writing with Sources*. This small, superb, and inexpensive book is the best one available, covering topics such as why you must cite, the basic principles of citing, the various forms of plagiarism (with examples), the misuse of sources, and the bad practices you must refrain from if you wish to stay in the clear.

5. Format

If you adhere to the formatting guidelines covered in this chapter, you will avoid annoying your instructors. You will send them a message that says, "I am a student who pays attention to the small details as well as the large ones." Note that because *The Chicago Manual of Style* (hereinafter, Chicago) is aimed at university faculty producing manuscripts for specific publishers who have their own formatting criteria, it has nothing to say on most of the following matters, which apply specifically to student papers.

TIPS FOR FORMATTING

5.1. Margins must be one inch on all four sides of the page. It is beyond shameful to fatten your margins because you don't have enough material to fill the allotted space.

5.2. The text must be doubled-spaced throughout, including long, "block" quotations. Do not use one and one-half spacing anywhere in the paper. With proper margins, there are roughly twenty-three lines of text on a double-spaced, 8½ x 11 inch-page, and about twenty-five lines on an A4 page.

5.3. Do not right-justify the text—leave it "ragged." If you right-justify, you produce a square block of text. It's true that paragraphs in books are right-justified, but book pages aren't more than eight inches wide. Don't produce a physical text that at best will make it difficult for your instructors to read and at worse will trigger migraines.

5.4. Have one blank line between paragraphs, not two. Hit the return key *once* when starting a new paragraph in a file that has been formatted for double-spaced text. This will automatically insert your one blank line.

5.5. Indent each new paragraph by roughly one half-inch.

5.6. Have one space between sentences, not two. (Two was required way back in the day when we used typewriters.)

5.7. The Modern Language Association (MLA) style guide allows the font size to range from 11 to 13 points while the American Psychological Association (APA) style guide goes with 10 to 12 (these numbers vary depending on the font style you use). Whatever you go with, ensure that the font is not so small it could make your instructors go cock-eyed, or so large that it feels like you're screaming at them.

5.8. I suggest using 12-point, Times New Roman font, which no instructor will find offensive.

5.9. If you have headings, and you are using MLA style, they should begin at the left margin, bolded, with uppercase and lowercase letters. The first sentence after a heading is left-justified.

Headings should look similar to the following (keep in mind that in your paper, all this text would be in "normal" font):

> *In order to draw out this point, it is necessary to move beyond the standard interpretations of how feudalism ended.*
> **The Origin of Capitalism**
> *Capitalism is a social relationship that...*

The example above works fine for Chicago style as well, but in APA, headings are centred and bolded while the paragraph immediately following the header is indented.

Note that if a heading is an orphan, sitting by itself on the last line of a page, you can bump it to the following page.

5.10. Insert page numbers in the top right-hand corner of the text.

5.11. In APA, page 1 is the cover page. In MLA, page 1 is the first page of the text (as there is no cover page).

5.12. If you are using Chicago style (which has no recommendation on covers for student papers), or you have not been instructed on what the cover of your paper must look like, you can use the following as a guideline. You should consider having:

(i) the title of the paper (near the top of the page);

(ii) your name (near the middle of the page); and

(iii) the course number and course name, the instructor's name, the name of the university, and the due date of the paper (all on separate lines, beginning near the bottom one-third of the page).

All this information should be centred, using both uppercase and lowercase letters. Do not use bold font and do not add any distracting text or images. I recommend having zero (0) as the number of your cover page, but don't show it (in Microsoft Word, click to remove the checkmark next to, "Show number on first page"). Page 1 then becomes the first page of text. See the sample cover below.

You Get What You Give:
The Case for Inequality

Mary Livingstone

SWRK 1006: Introduction to Social Work
Dr. Joan Rivers
Your University
12 March 2024

5.13. The cover for a student paper in APA format would look like the following, with the title boldfaced and all the information centred and clustered in the top one-third or so of the page.

Student papers in APA do not have headers or abstracts. Insert page numbers so they appear in the top right-hand corner.

> 1
>
> You Get What You Give: The Case for Inequality
>
> Mary Livingstone
> Department of Social Work, Your University
> SWRK 1006: Introduction to Social Work
> Dr. Joan Rivers
> March 12, 2024

5.14. In MLA format, student papers don't have cover pages (unless it's a group project with multiple authors). Rather, the required information appears at the top of the first page, and all of it is in plain font. It is left-justified except for the title, which is centred. You have a header with your surname and page numbers in the top right-hand corner. The introduction begins on the line after the title. It looks like this:

> Livingstone 1
>
> Mary Livingstone
> Professor Joan Rivers
> Introduction to Social Work
> 12 March 2024
>   You Get What You Give: The Case for Inequality
>   The first sentence of your opening paragraph is indented just like this. You then continue on to formulate your...

5.15. Learn how to incorporate numbers into your writing. In short, when do you use words, when do you use numbers, and when do you use a combination of the two? For instance, is it 40%, 40 percent, or 40 per cent? 12,000,000 dollars or $12 million?

5.16. If you are required to hand in a paper, print it single-sided (with the reverse side blank), unless you are instructed to print double-sided. Don't surround the paper with plastic or cardboard covers, which will end their days either rotting in a landfill or choking dolphins to death. Hold the paper together with a staple, or a paper clip if you don't have a stapler handy.

5.17. Unless otherwise instructed, do not attach any primary sources to your paper, such as photographs, newspaper articles, and brochures.

FURTHER READING

See chapter 1 ("Formatting Your Research Project") in the *MLA Handbook*, pp. 1–14; and chapter 2 ("Paper Elements and Format") in the *Publication Manual of the American Psychological Association*, pp. 29–49, with sample papers on pp. 50–67.

The conventions on writing with numbers vary slightly between Chicago, APA, and MLA. If you've been instructed to use a specific guide, then do so. If not, you will receive good advice from any of them. See *The Chicago Manual of Style*, chapter 9 ("Numbers"), pp. 589–618; the APA's *Publication Manual*, sec. 6.32 to 6.39 (pp. 178–81); and the *MLA Handbook*, sec. 2.126 to 2.139 (pp. 82–88).

PART II. *The Big Picture*

6. Title and Subtitle

Your paper should have an interesting title, preferably one that draws the reader's attention and almost implores them to investigate further. In this chapter, most of my examples consist of titles from academic journal articles found during a brief search on the web (they are included below in 6.4, 6.6 to 6.9, and 6.11 to 6.15). I have not mentioned authors' names as my objective isn't to call anyone out. If I had searched for a week or so, I could have easily found hundreds more examples, and any additional searching time would have generated thousands. My intent is to show that no aspect of a research paper is easy, including deciding what name you will give it. The goal is to learn from each other so we can improve our work.

TIPS FOR TITLES AND SUBTITLES

6.1. Do not have the assignment question as your title.

Is Socioeconomic Inequality Mostly Good or Mostly Bad for Society?

6.2. Do not have "Paper #1," "Thought Journal," or something similarly bland as part of your title.

6.3. Do not make your titles too short, something academics occasionally do. In a world where the number of journal articles published each year is now counted in the millions, many harried academics can't be bothered to download an article to discover what's behind some cavalier author's terse title. This disinclination applies to student papers as well. A vague title demonstrates a lack of concern for the reader, and it might annoy your world-weary instructor just seconds before they set eyes on your opening sentence.

Globalization and Civil Society

Feminism Again

Warm Weather Ahead

Social Disparities in Idaho

6.4. It's fine to have a title without a subtitle.

King Lear and the Irony of Blindness

Hell and the Cultural Evolution of Christianity

The Sustainability of an Anthropology of the Anthropocene

Program for a Transgender Existentialism

Gentrification and Social Classes in Paris, 1982–2008

6.5. Titles can come in the form of unanswered questions (with no subtitles), though those often have the whiff of clickbait, which the world can do without. I like titles that tell me what the issue is while also indicating how the issue will be approached.

Ok: *Is It Ethical to Use Medical Assistance in Dying?*
Better: *Medical Assistance in Dying: An Ethical Critique*

6.6. My preference is for titles that strongly hint at the main objective of the article.

How India's Ruling Party Erodes Democracy

The Seven Sins of Hunting Tourism

The Key Factors Contributing to the Persistence of Homelessness

Blundering Into Baghdad: The Right—and Wrong— Lessons of the Iraq War

6.7. Articles in the sciences go further, often having the main research findings as their titles. (These academics don't even pretend to flirt with their readers.)

Bells Reduce Predation of Wildlife by Domestic Cats (Felis catus)

Chronic Psychological Stress in Rats Induces Intestinal Sensitization to Luminal Antigens

Testosterone Causes Both Prosocial and Antisocial Status-Enhancing Behaviors in Human Males

FSH Blockade Improves Cognition in Mice with Alzheimer's Disease

6.8. If you have a subtitle, the title and subtitle combined should give us a general indication of the topic, the purpose of the paper, and/or its specific subject area.

How Soon We Forget: National Myth-Making and Recognition of the Armenian Genocide

Learning Regenerative Cultures: Indigenous Nations in Higher Education Renewal in Australia

Career Aspirations of Generation Z: A Systematic Literature Review

Working with "Monstrous Men": Ambivalent Sexism in the Bombay Film Industry

French Newsreels and the Suez Crisis: How to Make a Failure Look Like a Positive Outcome

(To maintain parallel phrasing, I would have changed the subtitle of the last example to *How to Make a Failure Look Like a Success*.)

6.9. If you have a subtitle, separate it from the title with a colon.

The Iraq War Ten Years On: Assessing the Fallout

6.10. If you have a title before a subtitle and it ends with a question mark or an exclamation point, omit the colon.

No: *Is Neoliberalism Dying?: A Review of the Literature*
Yes: *Is Neoliberalism Dying? A Review of the Literature*

However, add a colon if quotation marks come after a question mark or an exclamation point:

No: *"No way, man!" A Study of…*
Yes: *"No way, man!": A Study of…*

6.11. Titles can consist of a quotation with a subtitle adding specific details, though if you have a quotation, keep it brief, say four or five words. The following strike me as good uses of quotes; they add value to the title and pique our interest.

"I am not a religious crackpot": School Prayer, the Becker Amendment, and Grassroots Mobilization in 1960s America

"Press escape to skip concentration camp?": Player Reflections on Engagement with the Holocaust Through Digital Gaming

"Hairy honours of their chins": Whiskers and Masculinity in Early Nineteenth-Century Britain

"Can't jail the revolution": Policing, Protest, and the MOVE Organization in Philadelphia's Carceral Landscape

6.12. In contrast, it is often the case that the quotation is rather boring and the subtitle is way too long, as in the following made-up example.

"Here is a bland quotation that's going to get you geared up for a snoozefest": And Now Just to Irritate You Further I Will Add a Long Subtitle That Feels Like It Will Go on Forever and Ever and Ever

More seriously, in the following titles, I suggest the quotations aren't needed, because they don't add much or they produce a lengthy title/subtitle combination. The authors of these articles, I suspect, would disagree with my assessment—and you might as well. But whatever your opinion, I advise that you think twice before using a quotation as your title. It is becoming a tiresome academic trope.

Actual: *"To get freedom, one went abroad a lot": British Homosexual Men and Continental Europe as a Site of Emancipation, 1950–75*

Revised: *British Homosexual Men and Continental Europe as a Site of Emancipation, 1950–75*

Actual: *"After all our efforts at good citizenship": Propriety, Property, and Belonging in the Dispossession of Japanese Canadians, 1940s*

Revised: *Propriety, Property, and Citizenship in the Dispossession of Japanese Canadians in the 1940s*

Actual: *"They treat you like a person, they ask you what you want": A Grounded Theory Study of Quality Paid Disability Support for Adults with Acquired Neurological Disability*

Revised: *Quality Paid Supports for Adults with Acquired Neurological Disability: A Grounded Theory Study*

In the next example, my revision results in a title/subtitle longer than the original. The title also incorporates the "rule of three"; namely, that you can have three nouns in a series but should never have four or more.

Actual: *"There are lives here": The African and African American Cemeteries of the Bonnet Carré Spillway*

Revised: *Race, Ecology, and Commemoration: The African and African American Cemeteries of Louisiana's Bonnet Carré Spillway*

6.13. Avoid repeating a word (or a version of a word) in the title and subtitle. Here are some examples along with my suggested revisions:

Actual: *<u>Children</u> and the US Social Safety Net: Balancing Disincentives for Adults and Benefits for <u>Children</u>*

Revised: *Balancing Disincentives for Adults and Benefits for <u>Children</u>: The Case of the US Social Safety Net*

Actual: *Reproducing <u>Race</u> in the <u>Gentrifying</u> City: A Critical Analysis of <u>Race</u> in <u>Gentrification</u> Scholarship*

Revised: *<u>Race</u> and <u>Gentrification</u>: A Critical Analysis*

Actual: *<u>Career</u> Breaks, Broken <u>Pensions</u>? Long-Run Effects of Early and Late-<u>Career</u> Unemployment Spells on <u>Pension</u> Entitlements*

Revised: *Early- and Late-<u>Career</u> Unemployment Spells: The Long-Run Effects on <u>Pension</u> Entitlements*

Actual: *"It's a <u>lonely</u> old world": Developing a Multidimensional Understanding of <u>Loneliness</u> in Farming*

Revised: *Loneliness* in the UK Farming Community: A Multidimensional Understanding

Actual: The *War* in *Ukraine*: How Putin's *War* in *Ukraine* Has Ruined Russia

Revised: How Vladimir Putin's *War* in *Ukraine* Has Ruined Russia

6.14. It's necessary on occasion to repeat a word for effect. Sometimes this repetition borders on the poetic.

Home Sweet Home: The Emotional Construction of Places

Why Poor People Stay Poor

Going, Going, but Not Quite Gone

6.15. Don't have two subtitles, with the second one following a period, a question mark, or another colon. There are times in life when we just have to choose.

Actual: *Resilience as Part of Recovery: The Views of Those with Experiences of Psychosis, and Learning for British Mental Health Social Work Practice. A Scoping Review*

Revised: *Resilience, Recovery, and the Experiences of People with Psychosis: A Scoping Review*

Actual: *Food Banks and Food Security: Welfare Reform, Human Rights, and Social Policy. Lessons from Canada?*

Revised: *Food Security, Welfare Reform, and Human Rights in Canada*

Actual: *Divorce and Female Labour Force Participation: Do Women Who Expect an Upcoming Divorce*

Increase Their Employment? Evidence from Flanders

Revised: *Do Women Expecting to Divorce Increase Their Labour Force Participation? Evidence from Flanders*

FURTHER READING

For more suggestions, see chapter 6 ("Tempting Titles") in Helen Sword's *Stylish Academic Writing*, pp. 63–75.

7. The Introduction

The introduction is where you lay down the building blocks of your entire paper. You may be given specific guidelines on how to write an introduction; if so, follow them. For instance, papers in the sciences tend to have assigned sections: Introduction, Methods, Results, Discussion, and References. In these papers, my recommended three-paragraph introduction (consisting of a context, a thesis, and a road map), including the way I suggest you articulate your thesis, may have to be adapted to comply with the guidelines you receive. Introductions will differ depending on the discipline, so take what you find useful from my advice and add it to the requirements of whichever course you are in. A thesis is the only essential element of an introduction.

If you have not been given the specifics on how to formulate an introduction, then this chapter should serve you well. I suspect no instructor will be offended by your introduction if it looks like what I advocate for in this chapter. Indeed, after marking dozens of papers late into the night, as the candle burns to the size of a quarter and the recycling bin fills with empty wine bottles, any instructor who comes across your lucid, well-organized introduction might break into a smile thinking, "Yes, it *can* be done!" They likely will be relieved that they are about to read a paper that is the work of a careful, thoughtful writer.

An introduction should contain three components—a context, a thesis, and a road map—each of which is assigned its own paragraph. These paragraphs are a challenge to write. They consist of condensed versions of much larger thought processes, and because there is limited space available, you must use laser-precise wording. I recommend three paragraphs instead of a single lengthy one, to distinguish in your own mind the point of each component of your introduction. On your opening page, you are going to (1) draw readers in; (2) tell them what you will argue; and (3) tell them how your argument will unfold. If you have just one paragraph, even if these points follow in order, you are more likely to combine them, and so increase the probability that the introduction will devolve into a convoluted mess. It's okay, then, to break my three-paragraph rule, but if you do, you might be asking for trouble.

An instructor can spot that trouble, in the form of a poorly organized paper, almost immediately. The context consists of a couple of brief sentences. The thesis statement is barely visible, so there is no clear indication of the argument that will be made. The road map is hard to follow, or just not there. Together, these problems send a signal to an instructor that they are about to read the paper version of a car crash.

Instead, for a five-page paper, ensure that you assign roughly eighty to one hundred words to each of my components (so, 240 to 300 words total for the introduction). Overall, it should take up about three-quarters of the first double-spaced page. Anything less probably means you have not provided sufficient information to the reader, while anything more likely means you have provided too much. For longer papers, a general guideline is that the introduction should represent about 10 per cent of the total page count: one page for a ten-page paper, 1½ pages for a fifteen-page paper, and so on. In these introductions, the context and road map will be augmented only slightly compared to those in a five-page essay. You would use most of the extra space in your introduction (and in the paper itself) to detail your thesis. You likely won't have more arguments. Rather, you would expand on the justifications for each of your arguments, with greater depth of evidence.

CONTEXT

The context is the "hook" designed to invite readers into your paper, telling them why they should be interested in your topic, why it's important. You are essentially saying, "Pay attention, folks!" An effective way to approach the context is to tell a relevant anecdote, one that hints at what your thesis will be. Another way is to allude to a problem that has gone unsolved. Or you could refer to a question that most scholars, from your perspective, have failed to answer. You might also set up a debate, telling us the standard interpretation or dominant view of some event or theory. You would then proceed to challenge that interpretation/view in your thesis paragraph. (If you take the "debate" approach, you might need a citation or two in the context.)

TIPS FOR WRITING A STRONG CONTEXT

7.1. Don't have a context of, say, thirty or forty words; that's too brief. If that's all you have, then add a few sentences to elaborate on the story you are telling.

7.2. Don't have parts of the thesis (the justifications for the argument) mixed in with the context. You can't cover everything in your brief, opening paragraph. It's fine to simply suggest what your thesis will be, while not yet stating it outright or without incorporating any citations (they can come later).

7.3. Don't include definitions, like the following (they can also come later):

Inequality can be defined as "a situation where...."

According to the Oxford English Dictionary, *structuralism is "a theory that pieces of writing...."*

Capitalism has a division of social classes that...

7.4. Don't include detailed statistics, which are not appropriate for an introduction. This type of information can be moved into the body of the paper. You may, in contrast, provide a quick statistical summary, which a reader's mind can easily absorb.

> **No:** *The poverty rate for children in Nationia rose from 6.82% in 2012, then peaked at 8.42% in 2018, before falling to 7.17% in 2024.*
>
> **Yes:** *Why is it that one in every five people in the United Kingdom lives in poverty?*

7.5. Avoid quoting, unless it's just a small phrase consisting of a few words. The introduction (and the conclusion) are places in the paper where your own powerful voice must stand out.

7.6. Don't reach far back into history with a blanket statement that covers the entirety of space and time.

In olden days...

Since the beginning of time, people have always...

The world is billions of years old and yet...

In every society in history there have been...

As time changes and societies develop...

7.7. Situate the reader in a concrete physical *place* at a precise *moment*. When you begin with a phrase like *throughout history*, you toss the reader into a vacuum; we are nowhere at no point. (This advice on space and time should be applied to the rest of your paper as well.)

No: *In today's world, growing inequality is strongly prevalent and affects everyone.*

Yes: *In the United States, especially since the early 1980s, inequality has grown, and it has harmed especially those in the bottom 40 per cent or so of the population.*

7.8. The opening sentence of the context is especially important. You are like a singer opening their mouth to hit the first note, so make sure that that sentence entices the reader. Use short stories and fairy tales as an inspiration. Think of how your blood races when you read something like, "No one in the village went to the east end of the forest because that's where the monster lived." Okay, so in an academic paper it's not quite that simple. But you have to try. Students have great difficulty with opening sentences, but so do professors, journalists, bloggers, and anyone else who writes for a living. At the very least, avoid beginning with trite observations or banal generalizations.

7.9. Tell a story. To run a litmus test of your context, ask yourself: Will the reader see a picture in their mind when reading my context, in the same way that I pictured a monster hiding in a tree when I read the quoted sentence in the previous paragraph? Or have I left my readers to stumble over one abstract noun after another, preventing them from making an emotional connection with my topic? (And, yes, emotion is permitted in an academic paper, especially when it's your opening gambit.) Another benefit of telling a story is that it's easier to make the context flow, so you can avoid the bumpiness that occurs when writers are stuck and then try to cram too much into it. Tell a story, while holding the reader's hand, welcoming them into the paper.

7.10. Flip the narrative. For example, you could begin a paper on inequality by telling a story about the "American Dream," of big houses, big cars, and big hair. As the paragraph proceeds, a more troubling perspective is introduced, darkening the picture you began with, perhaps culminating with the death of a homeless person in your neighbourhood. The final sentence of the context would make clear that you find this situation distressing. You would leave us with the impression that for some people, the American dream is more of a nightmare.

7.11. The final sentence of the context provides a subtle link to the thesis. In a few words, you should be able to hint that there is something deficient with the status quo (whether that's a policy, a practice, a theory, an interpretation). At this point, you are inserting a *however* into the discussion, even if you don't use that word. Your argument will be made explicit in the thesis paragraph that follows.

> *With her diagnosis confirmed, Julie decided to access medical assistance in dying.*
>
> *It was the third time in the last seven years they had endured a "once in a century" flood.*

7.12. Look closely at introductory paragraphs in book chapters and journal articles and try to find some wonderful ones that will inspire you to compose wonderful ones of your own. If you do, you will discover how difficult it is to find stylishly written openings. And that's because they are so hard to write, even for seasoned academics.

THESIS

Whatever type of assignment question you receive, composing your answer as a *thesis*—an argument, your response to an encounter with a problem—will enable you to produce a paper that is more sophisticated than one without a thesis. This thesis is a clear statement of the main "truth claims" you are making, along with a succinct indication of the reasons, the justifications, for making these claims (this is the *why* of your thesis). The thesis must be subtle and sophisticated, not trivial or obvious. It must be "counter-arguable"; that is, it would be reasonable for someone to propose a view that is the opposite of yours. In a five-page paper, your thesis paragraph should consist of at least three well-developed sentences, so that you have one sentence for each of your major points. Doing this will help you to determine the order of your paragraphs and to figure out how these paragraphs might be structured.

The major drawback of most theses is the absence (or near-absence) of the *why*. Be sure to articulate in sufficient detail the reasons for your claims. Each sentence should have a word like *because*, which makes it clear that you are suggesting some type of cause-and-effect relationship between variables. These *because*-like words lead us into the *why* half of your sentences. The following is an example of how a thesis paragraph might begin:

> *This paper argues that the United States is the least democratic of the major capitalist countries because its laws create barriers to the formation of new political parties, promote voter suppression, and fail to adequately restrict campaign financing. Furthermore, the American political system encourages...*

Here's another example of a thesis sentence, suitable for an assignment defending the role of unions in socioeconomic life.

> *Second, unions increase workers' wages and improve their health and safety on the job, while allowing for more democracy in the workplace.*

Make your thesis as explicit as possible; leave the reader in no doubt as to what your argument will be. An academic argument is not akin to the plot of a mystery novel. If "the butler did it," then you must tell us so as part of the thesis statement on your first page. The rest of the paper will be the case you make—in this instance—to convince us how and why he "did it."

Be sure to draft your thesis as early as possible, once you have read even the beginnings of the literature. Modify the thesis with each successive draft. Check it for accuracy and precision before you polish the final version.

TIPS FOR WRITING A STRONG THESIS

7.13. In the opening sentence of the thesis paragraph, don't hesitate to use the expression, "In this paper, I argue that...." It is much better to use "I" than a cumbersome phrase like "this author." You could also go with, "This paper argues that...," if you want to refrain from using the subject *I* or the royal *we*. If you do, use this type of expression only as a transition into your thesis paragraph. Don't employ it anywhere else.

> *In this paper, I argue that socioeconomic inequality is mostly good for society as a whole.*

Avoid beginning the sentences that follow with unnecessary expressions such as, *In my view...,* or *I maintain that....*

> **No:** *In my view, democratic socialism is impossible to attain because...*
>
> **Yes:** *Democratic socialism is impossible to attain because...*

7.14. For a five-page paper, your thesis paragraph should lay out three powerful arguments (in three concise sentences). Don't combine the three arguments into a single sentence, such as: "Inequality has negative effects on early childhood education, physical health, and public safety"—and then leave it at that. Give each argument its due in its own sentence. So, in this instance, you might begin by addressing the question, "What are the precise, negative effects of inequality on early childhood education?" And then in sentences two and three you would ask the same type of question to yourself with regard to physical health and public safety.

7.15. Don't end your sentences too early. Finish each sentence with a clause that articulates the *why* of the matter. You want to give us a bit of information at this point—but not too much. If you say that inequality exacerbates social problems, tell us *which* social problems you have in mind. Fill in these details, otherwise your thesis will be vague.

> *Inequality harms physical and mental health because it _____, _____, and _____.*
>
> *Inequality affects schools, businesses, and families...* [how so?].
>
> *Inequality stigmatizes poor people...* [which results in them suffering... what exactly?].
>
> *In unequal societies, poor people face a number of challenges, including...*
>
> *Many wealthy people have influential roles in politics,* [*which gives them disproportional control of governments in our supposedly democratic societies*].

Note that adding the part in brackets in the previous example changes the sentence from an *observation*, which anyone can plainly see, to an *argument*, which helps us to understand what's problematic about what we are seeing.

7.16. Don't have overly bland sentences, which are a dead giveaway that you've conducted little research.

> *This paper will make the argument that inequality is bad, and it's a problem that we obviously must tackle at the current point in time, because we can see that as inequality gets worse we will just have some bigger problems we will need to face further on down the road.*

7.17. Don't have a thesis sentence that sounds like it belongs in your road map—one that has no argument and is just a list of topics that will be covered in the paper. That is, don't mix the road map in with the thesis (the justifications for the argument).

Inequality will be explained by examining social classes, private property, and rich-to-poor income ratios.

7.18. Argue along a continuum. In a paper on inequality, for example, you could propose that inequality is completely bad, somewhat bad, both bad and good, somewhat good, or completely good. In this case, don't pick "both bad and good" because you suspect it might be the safest place to sit. Pick it only if it will enable you to formulate the best evidence-based answer you can muster, the one you are most comfortable defending. You do not have to take an extreme position. A "centrist" argument is fine as long as you tell us you are going to make a centrist argument. If you do, though, don't try to convince us that both arguments are equally valid. That will be considered a cop-out on your part. If only slightly so, lean in favour of one argument over another, and tell us what ultimately served as the basis for your tie-breaking choice. Also, don't be afraid to opt for either end of the continuum—again, if this is where you find your intellectual home, and if you can marshal a compelling case as to why the rest of us should join you there. But keep in mind that the closer you are to one of the extremes, the more you will have to pay careful attention to counterviews.

7.19. Don't set up a "straw" argument, such as: "I am opposed to the idea that we should all be equal." Well, guess what? So is everyone else in the world. Making all humans perfectly equal is a view that no reasonable person would hold. Make your opponents' arguments as strong as *they* would make them—then you can critique them. A "straw" argument is a weak argument because you, in effect, have no opposition, no sensible, logical people to argue against.

7.20. Don't make a circular argument, one which basically says that "X causes X." These "theses" almost always amount to a *definition* of the term under discussion.

Inequality is bad because it's unequal.
Inequality promotes class hierarchy.
Inequality creates divisions in society.
Inequality leaves a gap between rich and poor.

7.21. Don't ascribe actions to *society*, but rather to certain individuals or groups in society. *Society* might just be the vaguest concept in the language. When I try to picture it in my head, I picture nothing.

Society continues to believe that...
Society has placed so much importance on...
For this reason, society needs to...
If society wants to change...
Globalization has many impacts on society.

The use of *society* is acceptable if you have given us the specifics of the society you are examining. In general, though, revise your sentences to get rid of it.

No: *Society tells us that White men are superior to other human beings.*
Yes: *A small group of wealthy White men developed the idea that...*

7.22. Don't ascribe actions to *history*.

No: *History informs us that prisons are...*
Yes: *A review of the history of prisons demonstrates that...*

7.23. Don't ascribe actions to *time*.

No: *The sixteenth century introduced new...*
Yes: *In the sixteenth century, English-language writers introduced new...*

7.24. Don't ascribe to *human nature* the supposed characteristics of every person who has ever existed. Over the last few decades, we've learned that human nature isn't all it's cracked up to be. So, be careful of claiming that certain actions, like aggression or competitiveness, are permanent and unalterable aspects of our being, while at the same time obliterating any references to the social, political, and economic contexts of our lives. There *is* something we can identify as "human nature," yet in the "nature vs. nurture" debate, scholars tend to assume that both are important. The question is always where we should place our emphasis, for any given characteristic (such as violence).

7.25. Don't mention your research materials. (You may have to in disciplines like psychology, but reserve that for the required "Methods" section.)

> *Through readings, statistics, and interviews, we will see that...*
>
> *Through the use of various academic sources, it will be shown that...*
>
> *As one examines the literature and research on teenage pregnancy, it becomes clear that...*

ROAD MAP

The road map indicates how the paper is organized, thus assisting the reader to follow along while also helping the writer to arrange their thoughts. The road map is a brief summary of the "stepping stones" of the argument—what issues will be covered and the order in which the discussion will unfold. It should have about three sentences, one for each of the major arguments you just made in your thesis paragraph. You need to say something like: "First, we discuss... Second, we examine... Next, we review... Finally, we determine...." The following is an example of one of these sentences:

> Second, we review differences in health outcomes between the United States and Sweden, focusing on life expectancy, infant mortality rates, and access to medical care.

In some ways, the road map mirrors the thesis, but it should not be a "copy and paste" version of it. Notice, for instance, that in the sentence above, it is *not* evident what the author will argue; that has been covered in the (preceding) thesis paragraph. And even if you were able to guess what the thesis is from this road map sentence, you would not know its specific details. So, if it seems like you are still making arguments in your road map, that the justifications for your thesis are getting a second airing, delete it and start over. The focus of the road map is solely on the issues that will be addressed. The body of the paper then follows exactly the plan laid out in this (third) paragraph.

I have seen suggestions that you probably don't need a road map in a short paper, especially if this road map is similar to the thesis statement. That's fine, but I maintain that the road map has a unique purpose. Its role is to tell us *what* you will survey in the course of demonstrating your argument.

TIPS FOR WRITING A STRONG ROAD MAP

7.26. It is a challenge, but try not to repeat phrases in the road map that you used in the thesis, otherwise the two paragraphs will be almost identical.

7.27. Don't begin the road map with a sentence like the following one. It tells us nothing and so is a waste of space in a paragraph that needs to be tightly written.

> There are many important issues we need to consider when analyzing inequality in our societies.

7.28. Don't tell us you will go into detail on something that is obvious.

We examine how those with larger incomes tend to lead more luxurious lives.

7.29. Do tell us something interesting, even surprising.

We demonstrate how wealthy people and corporations influence tax policy by…

7.30. Be sure to provide pertinent details in your road map sentences.

First, we examine how power is reinforced through institutions such as _____, _____, and _____.
Finally, we review the effects of discrimination on the health of racialized Americans, focusing on _____ and _____.

7.31. Write in the present tense, not the future tense. Technically, you are telling us something you *will* do, but the "doing" is so close, you may as well use the present tense and so drop a handful of *wills*.

No: *First, we will examine…*

Yes: *First, we examine…*

7.32. Go with *First, Second, Third* rather than *Firstly, Secondly, Thirdly*. Both are acceptable, but who needs that trio of "lees"?

7.33. Use different verbs. Don't say, "First, we discuss…," "Second, we discuss…," and so on. Use verbs such as *consider, demonstrate, describe, establish, explain, highlight, illustrate, review,* and *survey.* Never say *talk about.*

7.34. Have a subject (I recommend "we") and a verb near the *beginning* of every road map sentence. In the following example, *we* is our subject and *examine* is our verb.

First, <u>we examine</u> the role of unions in the postsecondary sector in the UK in negotiating for improved wages and benefits.

7.35. You are guaranteed to write a convoluted sentence that is difficult to follow if you don't have a subject like *we*. You will end up writing a passive sentence where the verb makes its appearance only near the end.

No: *Next, the case of inequality in Canada, which leaves millions of people in poverty, will be <u>discussed</u>.*

Yes: *Next, we <u>discuss</u> the case of inequality in Canada, which leaves millions of people in poverty.*

No: *First, the income gap between and within countries will be <u>noted</u>.*

Yes: *First, we <u>note</u> the income gap between and within countries.*

No: *Third, the effects on families of unequal access to health care will be <u>surveyed</u>.*

Yes: *Third, we <u>survey</u> the effects on families of unequal access to health care.*

Even worse, some of these passive "sentences" will be incomplete, mere clauses that cannot stand on their own.

Second, indicating the effects poverty has on opportunities to enter higher education.

Next, discuss the benefits of equality, noting its positive outcomes.

Last to be examined are the reasons why the rich exploit the poor.

7.36. Don't end the road map with a sentence full of fluff.

To conclude, we present a summary of the previous points.

In the end, this paper will have analyzed inequality of wealth while covering some of the positive and negative consequences of that inequality.

Instead, after positioning your road map's final stepping-stone, move immediately into the body of your paper, into your argument and your defence of that argument. When you have finished the next-to-last draft of the entire paper, review your road map to make sure you delivered on the promises you made to your readers.

FURTHER READING

For more helpful tips, see chapter 4 ("Introductions") in Gordon Taylor's *A Student's Writing Guide*, pp. 91–110.

8. Argument

The thesis statement governs the development and organization of your argument. The purpose of the information presented in what is sometimes called the "body" of the paper—the vast majority of your text—is to defend your thesis, your viewpoint. This thesis has to be supported by evidence so that the case is sophisticated and persuasive, where you also reflect on ideas, call assumptions into question, and challenge claims to truth. Overall, the paper must consist of a logical arrangement of ideas with an evident progression from the start, through the middle, to the end. It has to move from one point to the next, presenting step-by-step evidence, in an orderly manner with a clear sense of direction. You must not cast adrift a series of random thoughts, floating aimlessly with no intended destination, like a message in a bottle.

The argument you make in your paper derives from the assignment instructions. These will often begin with "task words" such as *analyze, assess, examine, explain, evaluate, critique, compare and contrast*, and so on. Make sure you are aware of what you are being instructed to do. If you are not clear on what the task word means, look it up in a good dictionary. In other instances, assignments are more open ended. You will be told, for instance, to "write a paper on any aspect of gun control policy in the United States." In all cases, however, you need to reframe the terms of your assignment into the central question—the thesis—that you wish to address, preferably a question that begins with *why* (though consult with your instructor on this). If you don't have a thesis, the resulting paper will lack focus.

To start, try to figure out which (two) positions are clashing in the assignment instructions, then choose one side in this clash, rather than simply "discuss" it, as the assignment might command. In effect, you pick a fight with other people, and your argument, at its bluntest, tells us why you and your fellow travelers are right and why those advocating for the other side are wrong. You will argue that your side is more coherent, more intellectually sound, or more ethical than the side you rejected, and you state in your thesis that you have chosen this side because of reason 1, reason 2, and reason 3.

In order to develop a solid argument, don't begin your thinking process by saying something like, "I'm writing a paper on gun control policy in the United States" (or on rap music, single mothers, or Islam). Ask a specific question that will require significant research to answer, such as: "Why do polls seem to show that most Americans want stricter control on guns but their governments continually fail to enact these controls?" *Now* you have the potential for an informative paper. There will certainly be controversy here. That's what you want. You take one side in a dispute and make a case, make an argument. From an instructor's perspective, these papers are always the most interesting to read.

An intriguing research question cannot be quickly answered with a *yes* or *no*. If you can answer a question immediately, before you read a sentence of research, then there's no argument to be made. "Is the moon made of green cheese?" No. So, there's nothing to write about. "Does socioeconomic status affect average life spans?" Yes—so again, nothing to write about. However, this question could be changed to "*Why* does socioeconomic status affect life spans?" This revised question is intriguing, especially if you live in a country that has "free," universal access to health care. Shouldn't Medicare equalize the life spans of rich and poor? What's up? Notice the element of mystery involved. A good question is a bit of a puzzle. The answer is not easy to discern. Your objective in your argument is to show why one answer is better than others, not why one answer is the *only* answer. You have to consider if sensible people would take the opposite view from the one you are arguing. If no one would, then you don't have a good question.

As you begin to write, don't type information on the page that fails to address your question. Do not pile on fact after fact, date after date, name after name, with no thought as to whether this helps you formulate an answer. Student papers sometimes have a lot of well-written, interesting material that provides little support for the thesis. "What does this have to do with my argument?" is a question you must ask yourself frequently as you write. So, you have to *choose*. You have to *prioritize* which issues will be discussed in detail and then assign those issues the appropriate amount of space in the paper. You must also show that you are not just summarizing but *analyzing*, providing us with insights that help us understand some phenomenon. You need to explain and defend the idea for which you are advocating.

As the paper progresses, much of what you originally planned is likely to change. Some sections will be moved, others will be dropped, and new ones will be incorporated. Some books and articles will be deleted from the bibliography, while others will be added. And so on. Your preliminary plans guide your approach; they are not a template to follow fastidiously. The paper will undergo numerous changes as you conduct further research and especially as you begin writing. Indeed, this process of discovery and rethinking is one of the main reasons why higher-level research can be so enjoyable.

TIPS FOR WRITING A STRONG ARGUMENT

8.1. Your argument builds on your thesis statement, which you should be able to summarize in a sentence or two. For example, *Capital punishment is not a deterrent to crime because....* Your argument is then a lengthy defence of that thesis. Always keep in mind what you are trying to demonstrate. This should be foremost in your thoughts, because all the evidence in the paper must somehow relate back to the thesis. Do not force your instructor to ask: "Why is *that* relevant?"

8.2. Think of your paper as in some ways resembling a defence lawyer's presentation in a court. To support your client, you must provide evidence. In the case of an academic paper, that evidence consists of facts, data, interviews, and testimonies, plus information extracted from written sources (newspapers, magazines) and especially from the writings of scholars (broadly defined), qualified with credentials, who are writing in their areas of expertise.

8.3. Understand the difference between an *opinion* and an *argument*. Opinion involves questions of taste, which you are not obligated to defend. You like vanilla ice cream; I prefer chocolate. An argument, on the other hand, requires a defence. "He is undoubtedly the worst president in U.S. history," you say. If someone asks you *why?*, an inadequate response would be: "He just *is*... and that's my opinion!" In any evaluation of a president's performance, we have left the realm of ice cream—with its likes and dislikes—and entered an argument which requires both sides to provide evidence to support their claims.

8.4. Tell us who is undertaking any action (who the "actors" are) and try to ensure we can picture them in our minds. Subjects we can visualize include: people—Norwegians, protestors, girls; animals—wolf packs, salmon, dogs; things—mountains, oceans, rain. We cannot picture *The iterations of postmodern subjectivity* *have...*; or *...where ongoing deprivations contribute to negative outcomes.* For sure, we can't have vivid actors in all our sentences, and perhaps not even in most of them, given that academic papers are frequently built around abstract concepts. Still, you should never miss an opportunity to have some actors, covered in flesh and full of blood, scattered throughout your paper.

8.5. When you are arguing for a cause-and-effect relationship, your actors (those who initiate actions) will typically be human beings, and they should be delineated as precisely as possible. An actor can be an individual (*Hitler overruled his...*); a group of individuals (*The miners' union fought back...*); or a corporate or state entity representing a clearly defined group of individuals (*Oxfam's press release revealed...*; *The Bolivian government pressured...*).

8.6. Sketch out your case in the form of a "tree diagram." The thesis is the trunk of the tree, each major argument is a large branch, and the sub-arguments are smaller branches (perhaps two or three of them) attached to each large branch. However you undertake this sketching, try to lay out the content of your argument. This sketch is completed before you attempt to write the paper and reworked as you revise it. If, like me, you are not a fan of (intellectual) trees, you might prefer an outline in the form of a linear list that runs down a page, with sub-arguments nested under each main argument (1a, 1b, 1c, 2a, 2b, etc.).

8.7. Question your "truth claims." Ask yourself: "How do I *know* this?" Make sure you don't just assert something without providing evidence, like those "people in the street" interviews on the local news. Instead, provide a solid foundation for your argument. That means dealing with opposition to the views you support.

8.8. Make accurate truth claims. If you were to argue that _____ *people on welfare are lazy*, which phrase would you use to fill in that blank? *All, Most, A majority of the, Half the, Some* *of the*, *A minority of the*, *Almost none of the*, or *None of the*? And what led you to this conclusion? In other words, how do you know this? Did you read a government's "Report to Taxpayers" or the rantings of an online blogger who lives in his parents' attic? Was your choice based on your prejudices (that is, your "prejudgments")? Or were you able to find more reliable sources to help make your decision?

8.9. Avoid exaggerating. For instance, saying something like, "Those born into the working class will remain there the rest of their lives" is problematic because it is inaccurate. You could amend the sentence by noting that it is possible for *some* folks to make it out of the working class, but that "only a few people" or "only a small fraction" do so. That sentence could be further improved with a precise statistic from a trustworthy source, which you would cite. If you exaggerate frequently, readers will ignore you at best and eviscerate you at worst.

8.10. Prioritize important points, giving each its due. Especially in a short paper, do not take a full page to drag out a relatively minor point which contributes little to the defence of the thesis. Do this in a half-page, a quarter-page, or even a sentence. This frees up room for you to raise further interesting and relevant issues. Even if you are developing a major point, try to make it concisely.

8.11. Do not make the error of glossing over crucial aspects of your argument. If something is important, expand on it, provide more detail. Recognize big ideas and give them plenty of room to breathe.

8.12. Avoid focusing almost exclusively on one or two points, even if they are great ones. They can almost certainly be condensed, leaving you space to address other relevant matters.

8.13. Be aware of what you are doing wherever you are in the paper. Be a *critic* of your own work. Ask yourself: What am I trying to accomplish? What is my purpose in this paragraph? Is this the best topic sentence I can write? Does the order of my thoughts make sense, or could I improve it by moving material around? Do I need three examples—perhaps one would do? And so on.

8.14. Don't focus too narrowly on the research materials. If you are asked to critique a 20-page journal article, don't pull all your ideas from two or three pages while ignoring everything else. If you do, you will repeat yourself frequently throughout the paper because you didn't conduct sufficient research. You won't have enough knowledge at hand. And that means you won't be able to propel the paper forward.

8.15. Be careful of relying too heavily on lecture notes. A very good regurgitation of the lecture will typically get you no more than a "C" (and sometimes much less than that). Your readers will wonder where the author disappeared to. Where are your thoughts, expressions, and analyses? Use lecture notes as a guide to help you develop your argument, not as something to send back to your instructors almost word-for-word. They already know what *they* think. They want to know what you think.

8.16. Make judicious use of statistics. Often, one statistic (rounded up to the nearest whole number!) is sufficient to support an argument. Writers, especially novice students, frequently drown their readers in mountains of data. "It was 6.17% in 1955, 6.23% in 1956, 6.19% in 1957, and blah, blah, blah." You will often need a detail or two to support a claim, but don't overdo it. Learn to hit the sweet spot.

8.17. An example (or anecdote) has to be representative of the evidence you are presenting. It must not be an exception you are trying to pass off as a rule. For instance, the destruction caused by a single serial killer should not be used to imply that all men are malicious, heartless beings.

8.18. Keep your personal life out of the argument. For example, don't have a long discussion about your difficulties accessing student loans and your worry about how you will repay them. That's a story to tell your friends at the pub. Research papers must be grounded in research. So, in this instance, you could peruse articles that survey and analyze loan recipients, looking at their emotional states, their financial situations after graduation, their default rates, and so forth.

8.19. Don't refer to yourself. We know you are an author with an argument. You announced your appearance in the introduction, especially in the thesis paragraph. We haven't forgotten you, so there's no need to send us a reminder. Your "I" is ever-present; the reader can still hear it even if you don't say it out loud.

No: *I believe* the war will only end when…

Yes: *The war will only end when*…

8.20. Don't try to be "objective," because there's no such thing. Instead, you must be *honest*. So, don't fabricate your data, misrepresent the ideas of other writers, or plagiarize.

8.21. Revise the text frequently. This means doing more than just rewording sentences, changing punctuation, and adding or deleting a few phrases. Do not be afraid to change major aspects of the argument as you write, by reconsidering ideas, rethinking the introduction and conclusion, adding and deleting evidence, and so on.

8.22. You may discover your thesis while drafting your argument. This is occasionally evident in papers where the main point comes at the end of the text. In such cases, this "thesis statement" needs to be moved to the beginning of the paper and the introduction needs to be reformulated. You would then proceed to defend the thesis throughout your revised and reorganized paper.

8.23. Read the draft with an eye to excising dispensable information. The limited space available must be used efficiently, with any weaknesses in the argument kept to a minimum.

8.24. If the paper is more than, say, eight pages, consider using headings to break it down into sections. This will force you to highlight and prioritize your argument.

8.25. Make sure your paper is not too short. If it is, it means you had more space available to develop new ideas and strengthen your argument. Any excessive brevity is proof of an inadequate effort on your part.

8.26. Make sure your paper is not too long. For sure, it is challenging to get all your evidence into a few pages, but that challenge is one of the purposes of short papers. They have been designed by your instructors specifically to see if you can select information, prioritize it, and condense it. Stay within the page limit set out in your assignment instructions. It may, however, be acceptable to go over by a few lines, say a quarter-page for a five-page paper.

8.27. Don't submit a paper—even a superbly written one—that is off topic, one that avoids dealing with the central question posed by your assignment.

FURTHER READING

More so than in any other chapter, this one has provided only the most basic tips. Because the quality of your argument is critical to the success of your paper, and given the complexities involved in developing and organizing an argument, you should make every effort to get your hands on the works noted below.

If you can afford to buy only one book from my bibliography, it should be Gerald Graf and Cathy Birkenstein's *"They Say / I Say."* I cannot recommend this book highly enough. It is reasonably priced, but if you are pinching pennies, any used edition from the second onward should serve you well. *"They Say / I Say"* is rooted in the idea that templates can help students organize their thoughts and improve their ability to formulate arguments. Each template asks you to figure out what others are arguing ("they say"), which you can then challenge with your own perspective ("I say"). These templates then become the foundation of your thinking. Once you construct that foundation by filling in the blanks, it becomes much easier to build the structure—the walls and roof, if you will—of your argument. Don't feel that templates might constrict your intellectual dexterity. Consider them training wheels for your brain. Your creative powers will blossom slowly over time, but only after you have mastered the basics.

For further helpful suggestions, see chapter 2 ("Reflection: Asking a Question and Proposing Answers") and chapter 5 ("Middles") in Gordon Taylor's *A Student's Writing Guide*, pp. 21–52 and 111–33; and *The Craft of Research*, by Wayne C. Booth et al., especially part 3 ("Making Your Argument") and part 4 ("Delivering Your Argument").

See also Anthony Weston's *A Rulebook for Arguments*, which has ten brief chapters containing fifty bite-sized rules, including "start from reliable premises," "reckon with counterexamples," and "detail objections and meet them." He also has an appendix explaining about two dozen common fallacies, including *ad hominem*, equivocation, false dilemma, and red herring. This small, inexpensive work should be on your bookshelf.

9. The Conclusion

The conclusion is a restatement of the argument you defended throughout the paper but without regurgitating what you already said. If you follow these guidelines, you will be able to separate your paper's conclusion from ones that are merely ordinary.

TIPS FOR WRITING A STRONG CONCLUSION

9.1. The conclusion should represent about 10 per cent of your paper, close to a half page (about 150 words) for a five-page paper, close to a full page for a ten-page paper, and so on.

9.2. The point of the conclusion is to reiterate why your argument matters. Your stance here might be more reserved than in the rest of the paper. Go for a modest ending—but don't grovel.

9.3. In your final paragraph, you are moving away from specific details and back up to a general level. So, don't try to cram everything you've argued into it. Focus on your most important points, which you might cover in the first sentence or two of the conclusion, and omit the evidence you already provided for these arguments.

9.4. Your final sentence should avoid clichés and should not try to tie everything together in a neat little bow ("And the world lived happily ever after!"). We do not want to hear violins playing and we don't want to taste something soaked in saccharine. Rather, leave us with a satisfying image, one that ranges anywhere from comforting to concerning to cataclysmic, perhaps one that reflects back on and mirrors the story you told in your context. In doing so, conclude with a compelling insight that puts the final touch on your argument. Consider the paper's opening and closing sentences as bookends.

9.5. You might think of your final sentence midway through your writing. Out of nowhere, it plants itself in your head. If so, type it into your draft as soon as you can, so you don't misplace it. You can always revise it later—or toss it out.

9.6. Do not use almost word-for-word duplications, a "copy and paste" of various sentences that appeared throughout the paper. This approach to writing the conclusion, where you employ language that is almost identical to what came before, is neither interesting nor innovative.

9.7. You can begin with a phrase such as *in brief, in conclusion, in sum, on the whole, to conclude*. Still, it's better if you can make a more creative link, one that's a bit cleverer, between the last sentence of your argument and the first sentence of your conclusion.

9.8. Do not introduce new and provocative ideas. If you do this while drafting the conclusion, either delete the ideas or expand on them in one of your body paragraphs.

9.9. While it's fine to have a small snippet of quotation—say four or five words—you should not rely on a relatively long quotation in the conclusion. It is important to hear your voice when you are finishing. Reserve quotations for your argument.

9.10. In some disciplines like psychology, you might give a nod to the need for further work that would address some of the shortcomings in the research that forms the heart of your paper.

9.11. Note that if your argument is not well developed, most likely the consequence of a lack of engagement with research materials, you will almost certainly have a weak conclusion, one that tells us little of importance. Strong arguments generate strong conclusions.

FURTHER READING

For more tips, see chapter 6 ("Endings") in Gordon Taylor's *A Student's Writing Guide*, pp. 134–44.

10. Citations

You must cite your sources consistently and accurately to indicate to readers where you have obtained the information and evidence used to build your argument. In this chapter, I provide sample references for Chicago, MLA, and APA citation styles for books, journal articles, and chapters in edited books ("edited collections"), and I also show you how to cite your sources in the text or in footnotes/endnotes. There are hundreds of other types of research sources I won't cover, including translations, newspaper articles, book reviews, films, poems, blogs, podcasts, and skeets. Under Further Reading, I will let you know where you can find the information needed to cite them.

There are many differences between citation styles, for instance, in the order of names in multi-authored works, the use of authors' first names (or initials), whether quotation marks are required for article titles, the forms of capitalization in titles, and so on and so on. Because each citation style has its own innumerable idiosyncrasies, using one with which you are not familiar requires an almost Zen-like attention to detail. And be aware that these details are yet another indicator of the quality of your work. I am not exaggerating when I say that my first glance at a student's references list strongly suggests whether I am about to read a paper that is a superb "A," a solid "B," a mediocre "C," or a disastrous "D" or "F."

BIBLIOGRAPHY + FOOTNOTES/ENDNOTES: CHICAGO MANUAL OF STYLE

The following examples show how each work appears in a bibliography and how it appears in a footnote or endnote the first time it is cited. I also show how it is cited again, after the full citation (Chicago recommends avoiding *ibid.*), by employing the author's surname and a "short" title. The page number(s), when you have one, is placed at the end of a note. For these citations, a matching superscript number would appear somewhere in the sentence, usually at the end like this.[1]

Book

BIBLIOGRAPHY

Kooser, Ted. *The Poetry Home Repair Manual: Practical Advice for Beginning Poets.* University of Nebraska Press, 2007.

FOOTNOTES/ENDNOTES

1. Ted Kooser, *The Poetry Home Repair Manual: Practical Advice for Beginning Poets* (University of Nebraska Press, 2007), 54.
2. Kooser, *Poetry*, 35.
3. Kooser, *Poetry*, 81.
4. Matthew Zapruder, *Why Poetry* (Ecco, 2018), 159.
5. Kooser, *Poetry*, 142.

Journal Article

In the following example, the article is found in volume 46, issue number 2, of the journal *Teaching Philosophy*.

BIBLIOGRAPHY

Rodier, Kristin, and Samantha Brennan. "Teaching (and) Fat Stigma in Philosophy." *Teaching Philosophy* 46, no. 2 (2023): 189–207.

FOOTNOTES/ENDNOTES

1. Kristin Rodier and Samantha Brennan, "Teaching (and) Fat Stigma in Philosophy," *Teaching Philosophy* 46, no. 2 (2023): 196.
2. Rodier and Brennan, "Teaching," 191.
3. Rodier and Brennan, "Teaching," 200.
4. Kate Manne, "Humanism: A Critique." *Social Theory and Practice* 42, no. 2 (2016): 394.
5. Rodier and Brennan, "Teaching," 203.

Chapter in an Edited Book

In the following example, Joy Williams is the author of the chapter, "The Psychopaths" is the title of the chapter, John Freeman is the editor of the book, and *Tales of Two Planets* is the title of the book.

BIBLIOGRAPHY

Williams, Joy. "The Psychopaths." In *Tales of Two Planets: Stories of Climate Change and Inequality in a Divided World*, edited by John Freeman. Penguin, 2020.

Note: Chicago does not require page numbers in the bibliography for a chapter in an edited book.

FOOTNOTES/ENDNOTES

1. Joy Williams, "The Psychopaths," in *Tales of Two Planets: Stories of Climate Change and Inequality in a Divided World*, ed. John Freeman (Penguin, 2020), 255.
2. Williams, "Psychopaths," 257.
3. Williams, "Psychopaths," 257.
4. Lindsey German and Nina Power, "A Feminist Manifesto for the 21st Century," in *Burn It Down! Feminist Manifestos for the Revolution*, ed. Breanne Fahs (Verso, 2022), 199.
5. Williams, "Psychopaths," 256.

REFERENCES/WORKS CITED + IN-TEXT CITATIONS

For the following three in-text referencing systems, every reference cited in the text must be in a list of references or works cited, and every item in one of these lists must be cited in the text at least once. For each style, I include an example of how to cite Ted Kooser's book (which you can replicate for any research source), showing the two ways of citing. These are *parenthetical*, where all the relevant information is in parentheses in the text, and *narrative*, where the author's name is integrated directly into your text.

Chicago Manual of Style

REFERENCES/WORKS CITED LIST

Kooser, Ted. 2007. *The Poetry Home Repair Manual: Practical Advice for Beginning Poets*. University of Nebraska Press.

Rodier, Kristin, and Samantha Brennan. 2023. "Teaching (and) Fat Stigma in Philosophy." *Teaching Philosophy* 46 (2): 189–207.

Williams, Joy. 2020. "The Psychopaths." In *Tales of Two Planets: Stories of Climate Change and Inequality in a Divided World*, edited by John Freeman. Penguin.

IN-TEXT PARENTHETICAL

… from the soul (Kooser 2007, 54).

IN-TEXT NARRATIVE

According to Kooser (2007, 54), the…

Modern Language Association (MLA)

REFERENCES/WORKS CITED LIST

Kooser, Ted. *The Poetry Home Repair Manual: Practical Advice for Beginning Poets*. U of Nebraska P, 2007.

Rodier, Kristin, and Samantha Brennan. "Teaching (and) Fat Stigma in Philosophy." *Teaching Philosophy*, vol. 46, no. 2, 2023, pp. 189–207.

Williams, Joy. "The Psychopaths." *Tales of Two Planets: Stories of Climate Change and Inequality in a Divided World*, edited by John Freeman, Penguin, 2020, pp. 253–57.

IN-TEXT PARENTHETICAL

Some good advice for a poet is "to write from your soul no matter what form you choose because that's what really matters" (Kooser 54).

IN-TEXT NARRATIVE

Ted Kooser urges poets "to write from your soul no matter what form you choose because that's what really matters" (54).

American Psychological Association (APA)

REFERENCES/WORKS CITED LIST

Kooser, T. (2007). *The poetry home repair manual: Practical advice for beginning poets*. University of Nebraska Press.

Rodier, K., & Brennan, S. (2023). Teaching (and) fat stigma in philosophy. *Teaching Philosophy*, 46(2), 189–207.

Williams, J. (2020). The psychopaths. In J. Freeman (Ed.), *Tales of two planets: Stories of climate change and inequality in a divided world* (pp. 253–57). Penguin.

IN-TEXT PARENTHETICAL

...for those just learning how to write poetry (Kooser, 2007, p. 54).

IN-TEXT NARRATIVE

Kooser (2007, p. 54) advises that...

TIPS FOR CITING

10.1. Be sure to scrupulously follow the citation system required as per your assignment instructions and try to reduce the number of errors to a minimum. If you are permitted to choose a system, pick the one you are most comfortable with.

10.2. In a five-page paper, have roughly ten to fifteen citations, about two or three per page, to give a clear indication of your sources. Having only a handful of citations may raise eyebrows, leading your instructor to wonder if you read much. Having too many, say over twenty-five, might be seen as a case of too much information. All academic writers should follow the advice provided by *The Chicago Manual of Style* (sec. 13.5), which suggests that, "in general, readers are better served by a disciplined, focused approach to source citations than by one that treats citations as a repository for every scrap of information consulted during the course of research and writing."

10.3. In disciplines like psychology, page numbers are included usually only when quoting. The in-text citations typically exclude these numbers, because it is the entire work, its main finding or discovery, that is under discussion.

> *Jones (2021) concludes that children subjected to trauma during the Syrian civil war…*

10.4. In many other disciplines, it's quite different. Because you are often focusing on the particularities of an author's argument, or summarizing a few pages of their text, your default should be to have a page number (or numbers) for nearly every citation. If no citations (or just a few) direct us to specific pages, it looks suspicious, as if you are trying to hide something.

> *Andrews and Smith (1981, 12) argue that the most important…*

10.5. Your Notes, Works Cited, References, and/or Bibliography must begin on a new page.

10.6. Even if you use an in-text referencing system, you might occasionally want to have a few notes where you elaborate on issues raised in the text, add something that is slightly tangential, provide overly technical information, and so on. In doing so, use Arabic numerals (1, 2, 3, etc.), not Roman numerals (i, ii, iii, etc.), and format them in "superscript." In North America, the numerals are usually placed at the end of the sentence, "like this."[1] If you are in the UK, it would be 'like this'.[1] In your paper, begin any endnotes (Notes) on a separate page, after the main text and before the references, bibliography, or works cited.

10.7. For each book, list the publisher not the copyright holder—identified next to the symbol ©—though note that occasionally the publisher and the copyright holder are one and the same.

10.8. If you have used a chapter from an edited book, then have a citation that includes the author(s) and title of the chapter, and not merely the editor(s) and title of the book.

10.9. Do not have a "padded" list of references, one that includes a number of items you do not cite in your paper. Instructors throughout the world concur that padding is both sad and risible.

FURTHER READING

See Gordon Harvey's *Writing with Sources*, pp. 56–118, which gives a succinct summary of the MLA and APA in-text referencing systems; Chicago style, when using a bibliography (and footnotes or endnotes); and the in-text and citation-sequence styles of the Council of Scientific Editors.

If you are in North America, you may want to purchase one of the three standard citation guides (Chicago, MLA, or APA) as you advance through your undergraduate degree and settle on a major. You may also find these guides in the form of ebooks in your library's collection. Either way, if you plan to pursue graduate studies in the social sciences or the humanities, it will be essential for you to have easy access to whichever guide you use regularly.

If you are in the United Kingdom, consider purchasing *Cite Them Right* by Richard Pears and Graham Shields. It covers

Harvard style in detail, over roughly ninety pages. In addition, in chapters of about twenty pages each, it highlights a number of referencing systems, including Chicago, MLA, APA, Vancouver, the Modern Humanities Research Association, the Institute of Electrical and Electronics Engineers, and Oxford's system for legal citations.

PART III. *The Mechanics of Writing*

11. Paragraphs and Sentences

The organization of your writing, the way you present your thoughts, is crucial to the success of your paper. The paragraph is the most important building block of writing. It is a collection of sentences that convey one idea only. This idea forms the basis of an appropriate topic sentence (a general statement, or "mini-thesis," that controls the information in the paragraph), a sentence that makes a promise to the reader, informing us of the topic you are about to discuss. The sentences that follow support and elaborate on that mini-thesis. The paragraph moves from the general to the specific (providing details, evidence, data), before shifting back up to a general level in a sort of summary of what we've just read. In contrast, a confused paragraph discusses a number of unrelated issues, most of them with little connection to the topic sentence. When this happens, it seems that the author has forgotten the point they were trying to make.

This is why a good topic sentence is critical to the formation of a paragraph. The following is one example: *Sweden has designed a welfare system that serves to protect its citizens from the negative effects of the free market.* Notice how this sentence sets up a feeling of *anticipation* in the reader, who will surely want to know more: What are the features of this system? How did these features come about? What makes them so positive? And so on. This general topic sentence works because a paragraph is like an inverted triangle (▽), moving from a broad, wide-ranging beginning to a more pointed, specific ending. An example of a bad topic sentence is, *Workers' Compensation was introduced in Sweden in 1901 and was made compulsory by 1916.* This sentence is too specific, too "factual." Notice how it basically shuts down discussion; what else is there to know? That sentence is still useful, though. It just needs to appear in the middle of the paragraph, not at the beginning.

The paragraph I just described, with the topic sentence first, is a template. You would not want all your paragraphs to look like this, especially in a paper of more than, say, five pages. But if you are having difficulty expressing your thoughts, you may want to stick with the template. The topic sentence does not have to be the lead sentence in a paragraph, but be careful if you move it elsewhere. Perhaps hold off on experimenting until you are fairly confident in your writing abilities, when you feel more in control of what you are putting on the page.

You must also be aware of what is happening within paragraphs, where sentences have to link, flowing smoothly from one to the next, with no leapfrogging from one idea to another. Ideas must not become unhinged, unconnected to what comes before or what comes after. Rather, there needs to be a sensation of *gliding* from point to point. When it's not done properly, the feeling is one of lurching back and forth, like being on a bus where the driver is constantly pumping the brakes.

Paragraphs also have other essential features. Their sentences are complete and grammatically correct; word choices are appropriate and precise. For the most part, the author uses an active voice. Spelling is accurate; the text has been proofread a number of times. The punctuation is near flawless, especially the use of commas and semicolons. In sum, you must write with care. Any mistakes you make will distract readers and throw them off. Think of them walking on a balance beam; they don't need you poking them in the ribs with a sharp stick, ruining their concentration and knocking them off their stride.

TIPS FOR WRITING STRONG PARAGRAPHS

11.1. Understand the *objective* behind each paragraph. Are you describing something? Illustrating a point? Comparing two phenomena? Arguing over a definition? Trying to explain why an event happened? Classifying ideas to see how they are related?

11.2. Paragraphs must follow each other in a logical manner. Do not present your arguments to the reader arbitrarily, in the order that you first thought about them, as if you just sat at the computer and typed everything from beginning to end (the infamous "night before job"). Give some thought to how you will arrange your materials. For instance, in a paper that is organized chronologically, don't move from, say, the 1920s to the 1970s, then back to the 1940s, then forward again to the 1990s unless you have a clear reason for doing so. If your paper is organized thematically (as most papers are), you should move from the general to the specific, from the broad to the narrow, so you first draw the "big picture" then home in on the details. For example, in a paper on homelessness, you could begin by discussing the competition and profit maximization that are at the heart of capitalism (a macro issue), then move to an analysis of how housing markets work (a mezzo issue), then end by pointing out the absence of sufficient homeless shelters in your community (a micro issue).

11.3. If your paragraphs are unified and follow each other in a sensible manner, then when your paper is finished, someone should be able to read the introduction, the first sentence in each paragraph, and the conclusion, and have a general understanding of your work. They should be able to see, hear, and comprehend the story you are telling, the argument you are making. Read the topic sentences to check the flow of your writing. One of the benefits of doing so in other people's work is to quickly grasp the central ideas of their writing. But then you have to apply this same standard to yourself. If you write this way, thinking about your topic sentences, it will force you to clarify the organization of your argument. This will prevent you from composing several pages with little or no point to them. You will also avoid repeating yourself, while keeping in mind the formula: one point = one topic sentence = one paragraph.

11.4. When you move to your next topic, begin a new paragraph and provide a "bridge" or a link between these paragraphs to connect your thoughts. The reader needs to know: Why are we discussing this (new) issue at *this* stage in the argument? Don't move too quickly from one issue to the next. For instance, you could begin a paragraph with, *Power is the ability of one individual or group to control...*, but this sounds like a definition. And if all your topic sentences are similar to that one, the resulting paper will be a mere listing of unrelated and disconnected points instead of an integrated collection of ideas. A better bridge would be, *Power is another aspect of social life that limits our ability to be truly individual.* The bridge here is *another*, whereby you signal to your reader that a transition is underway. It links this new paragraph to the preceding discussion. The reader can see where we are headed. Also, *limits our ability to be truly individual*, we can assume, is a nod to the author's thesis statement. Do not undertake this bridging in an overly mechanical manner, however. For example, the next paragraph in this essay should not begin with, "And *yet another* aspect of social life that limits...." The trick is to avoid a series of links that are almost formulaic, such as:

Firstly, / Secondly, / Additionally, / Furthermore, / Consequently, / Lastly, / In summary,

The first feature... / The next feature... / The final feature...

> *The third reason justice will...*
> *Another argument for...*
> *Now, this paper will look at...*
> *This brings me to the following point...*

You can use these types of links sparingly (as in my example, when I used *another*), though for the most part, paragraphs should be linked almost surreptitiously, so we hardly notice you've made a connection. Strive to make each link seamless, like a beautiful garment; you can't tell how it holds together unless you look closely and stare at it. In contrast, if you often say, in effect, "I just talked about *that* and now I'm going to talk about *this*," you will produce written hiccups that jar the reader.

11.5. When bridging paragraphs, use words like *this* or *these* or "adding words" like *also, furthermore, in addition, likewise, moreover, next, similarly,* or *still* (though don't overuse these adding words). You can also repeat a keyword or a close relative of that word used in the previous paragraph. It does not need to be in the last sentence of the paragraph, but it should be prominent, perhaps an important concept that's under discussion. Another option is a "half and half" sentence, one that looks back as well as ahead. In the following example, we assume that the "stents" have been introduced to the reader (the look back), while the second half of the sentence (the look ahead) promises to further the story.

> *Although his stents slowed him down somewhat, he wasn't done yet.*

11.6. Think of the last sentence in the paragraph as the exit ramp, moving away from the main point of your topic sentence. Your final thought reflects on what you just said; it does not initiate your next idea. That job of transitioning is assigned to the topic sentence of the following paragraph.

11.7. One common bridging flaw is when the writer locates the topic sentence as the last sentence of the previous paragraph. This problem is easily solved—just bump the sentence to the beginning of the next paragraph. A similar flaw involves repeating the last few words of the final sentence in a paragraph as the opening few words in the first sentence of the next paragraph. You should be more creative than that. So don't do it like this:

> *...while the second aspect required the elimination of democracy.*
> *This elimination of democracy...*

11.8. If you are finding it difficult to connect your paragraphs, you likely need to reorder the discussion to improve the flow. It also suggests that you don't have a "story arc," a series of linked scenes of the kind you expect to see when watching a movie and we expect to hear when reading your paper.

11.9. Headings in a small paper of, say, less than seven pages are often used as a lazy way to link paragraphs, sidestepping the difficult work of producing successful bridges. As a result, you should avoid them, because their presence will give the paper a choppy feel, thus interrupting the flow.

11.10. There is no magical length for a paragraph. A rough guide would be about two paragraphs per typed, double-spaced page, so if one of yours exceeds much more than a half-page, warning bells should be going off telling you it's time to wrap up. Paragraphs seem to have a natural rhythm, almost akin to a three-minute pop song, the length of which strikes us as just about right. Anything much shorter, say around two minutes, makes us feel almost cheated (unless it's a masterpiece like The Beatles' "Eleanor Rigby"). Anything longer, say around four minutes, might make us impatient. To avoid antagonizing us, the song needs to introduce something new—be it lyrics, vocals, or instruments—that almost demands that we remain attentive, as opposed to repeating the chorus for the fourth or fifth time. Anything beyond four minutes is likely to have our brains screaming, "shut that thing off!" (unless it's a masterpiece like The Beatles' "Hey Jude"). In contrast, a delightful rhythm in a paragraph of appropriate length pleases the ear and comforts the eye. Think of your paragraphs as songs, as little works of art that should come in perfectly sized packages.

11.11. Avoid paragraphs that are too long, that ramble on for what seems like an eternity as the writer abandons the topic sentence while bouncing aimlessly from one idea to another. Few students can maintain the momentum of a paragraph if it extends to more than a page, never mind the two- or even three-page behemoths I have occasionally encountered. These paragraphs almost always contain more than one key idea. Do a visual scan of your various drafts to ensure that paragraphs, with rare exceptions, are kept to about half a double-spaced page, three-quarters at most. Ask yourself if the topic sentence refers to everything discussed in the rest of the paragraph. If it doesn't, then revise. Sometimes, you need only hit the *return* key to start a new, reasonably coherent paragraph. But more likely, there's too much going on and it's mostly scattershot. Reading this kind of writing makes me feel like a blind cat whose human has just moved the furniture. Even worse is a whole paper consisting of 1½-page paragraphs. If you write like this, you will brutalize your readers who will respond accordingly by dreaming of better days to come.

11.12. Avoid paragraphs that are too short, that have only one or two brief sentences. If the point made is important, you need to expand on it. If not, it's probably insignificant, and should be dropped. Once your paper is drafted, do a visual scan to see if you have any stunted paragraphs and, if so, either develop them further or delete them. Keep only those that you have purposefully left short, perhaps to elicit an emotional reaction from the reader by highlighting some critical piece of information in a handful of words.

TIPS FOR WRITING STRONG SENTENCES

11.13. Watch your verb tenses. Avoid constantly shifting back and forth between tenses. This movement makes your writing irritating to read and your argument difficult to follow. Whatever tense you choose, be consistent. Obviously, there will be times when changing tenses is necessary in order to make sense, but try to keep this shifting to a minimum.

11.14. Different verb tenses are used for different purposes. If you are discussing debates, even if they occurred long ago, use the present simple tense.

Marx <u>criticizes</u> Hegel for failing to account for…
Adam Smith <u>argues</u> that workers' wages are…

If you are discussing debates that are ongoing, use the present perfect tense (*has* or *have* + the past participle of the verb).

Many scholars <u>have argued</u> that the postmodern turn…

If you are discussing an event which occurred at a specific moment, use the past tense.

Marx and Engels <u>wrote</u> The Communist Manifesto in 1848.

11.15. Choose your verbs carefully. Does each sentence use a precise verb? Do these verbs mean what you think they mean? If you repeatedly choose the wrong verb, your writing will be blanketed by an impenetrable fog. Readers can sort of see where they are going, but you've made the seeing needlessly complicated for them.

No: *It <u>imposes</u> the government to…*

Yes: *It <u>requires</u> the government to…*

11.16. Keep your subject and your verb close together. Here is an example of what happens when you ignore this advice, from an article published by the Associated Press.

> <u>Barbara Walters</u>, *the intrepid interviewer, anchor and program host who blazed the way as the first woman to become a TV news superstar during a career remarkable for its duration and variety,* <u>has died</u>. *She was 93.*

The long sentence contains an astounding thirty words between the subject (*Barbara Walters*) and the verb (*has died*). The sentence would have been especially upsetting to those who trundled through that lengthy interrupting phrase thinking that maybe Ms. Walters had won the lottery. As a result, it probably would have been better if the two sentences had been written as follows:

> <u>Barbara Walters</u> <u>has died</u> *aged 93. She was an intrepid interviewer, anchor, and program host who blazed the way as the first woman to become a TV news superstar during a career remarkable for its duration and variety.*

Here's another example from a book on anarchism, published by Penguin:

> *Europeans had absorbed the wisdom of the East—metallurgy, the domestication of animals, written language, industry, arts, science, metaphysics, religion and mythology—<u>to establish pre-eminence</u>.*

This use of dashes is common, yet in many instances, including this one, they can be eliminated. If we take the last phrase and move it to the beginning of the sentence, it reads as follows:

> *To establish pre-eminence, Europeans had absorbed the wisdom of the East, including metallurgy, the domestication of animals, written language, industry, arts, science, metaphysics, religion, and mythology.*

Furthermore, because the examples of wisdom all seem to carry equal weight, I would have revised the sentence again to improve the rhythm (and produce an alliteration from the three m-words), rearranging the wisdoms from the shortest (in terms of syllables) to the longest, perhaps something like this:

> *To establish pre-eminence, Europeans had absorbed the wisdom of the East, including arts, science, industry, religion, mythology, metaphysics, metallurgy, written language, and the domestication of animals.*

In sentences, you can sometimes have a verb at the end, perhaps because you want to build suspense, keeping us on our toes. That is, you need a good reason to hold back the *subject + verb* combination, because it helps to ground your readers. If you are going to suspend us in mid-air, in the sentence version of a comedian's joke, through clause after clause, the "punchline" had better be worth it.

11.17. Try to reduce the use of the verb *be* (*am, is, are, were, was, been, being*). This often entails deleting the *be* form and cutting an *-ing*.

Ok: *She is running*.

Better: *She runs*.

One problem with *be* forms is that they can make it unclear what you are referring to, for instance, when you begin sentences with *It is* or *This was*. In your paper, you can't root out all the uses of *be*, and perhaps not even most of them, but look closely at the places where *be* produces vagueness and especially where it makes for lethargic sentences.

11.18. While disciplines like mathematics are built around the notion of "proofs," in the social sciences and the humanities you should avoid saying you *proved* an argument. Find a more modest verb instead.

No: *My analysis proves that...*
Yes: *My analysis suggests that...*

11.19. Maintain a parallel grammatical structure throughout each sentence.

No: *She was smiling, laughing, and cried at the same time.*
Yes: *She was smiling, laughing, and crying at the same time.*

11.20. Avoid passive sentences as much as possible. They usually have the doer of the action appear near the end of the sentence, which typically contains some version of the verb *be* (often *was* or *were*) and the prepositions *by* or *of* (*The house was built by Jack*). These sentences make it difficult to discern who the actor is—the person or persons performing the action, someone we can easily picture in our minds. A series of passive sentences can cause confusion for your readers, who must struggle to understand how ideas relate to each other. Passive sentences also make it more likely that you, the writer, will get lost. To address these problems, find your human beings (your subjects) and move them closer to the beginning of each sentence, so we can immediately comprehend who the driving force is behind the action that your verb will announce (*Jack built the house*).

Compared to passive sentences, active sentences are more vibrant and are easier for readers to follow. Still, it is perfectly fine to employ some passive sentences. There are times when you want to be quiet and gentle. But don't overuse the passive voice. Default to the active mode when sentences call for action and vigour.

11.21. Avoid having too many short sentences, which will make your work feel jittery. Try to join closely related thoughts into a single sentence. Avail yourself of commas, semicolons, and words like *however, therefore, hence,* or *nevertheless*. Reserve short, pungent sentences especially for key points in the argument, where they might serve as the well-mannered writer's equivalent of pounding a fist on the table.

Patriarchy lifts men up and pushes women down.
The world is on fire and we're watching it burn.

11.22. Don't have any sentence fragments (incomplete sentences). They are either lacking a subject and/or a verb, or they are dependent clauses.

No: *We had a great view. Because we lived in a house on a hill.*

Yes: *We had a great view because we lived in a house on a hill.*

You might occasionally add a fragment in here and there as part of the rhythm of a paragraph, but if you attempt this, you need to know what a fragment is and why you are using it.

11.23. Your sentences should convey a confident authorial voice.

No: *Capitalism is <u>known to be</u> unfair and discriminatory.*
Yes: *Capitalism is unfair and discriminatory.*

In the "yes" sentence, the author makes it clear that they are staking an ownership claim in this argument. The author of the "no" sentence seems to agree with the argument but isn't quite ready to embrace it with an effusive bear hug. The wording is vague enough that that author might even reject the argument, clarifying that they meant, "It's known to be unfair and discriminatory by *other* people but certainly not by me!"

11.24. Don't begin a sentence with *Which*.

No: *She ate the large green apple. Which was sitting on the counter next to the toaster.*

Yes: *She ate the large green apple, which was sitting on the counter next to the toaster.*

11.25. Don't begin a sentence with *Meaning*. If you need to explain what you just said ("by that I mean ..."), then you didn't explain it properly in the first place. Go back and rewrite the text or perhaps join two sentences with *which*.

No: *The policy forced people to shelter in place. Meaning that it resulted in a loss of business for the store.*

Yes: *The policy forced people to shelter in place, which resulted in a loss of business for the store.*

11.26. Avoid needlessly repeating the same word. Unintentional repetition in writing produces the musical equivalent of a monotonous drumbeat. For example, for *welfare* substitute *social assistance*, *government support*, or *public programs*. Purchase a thesaurus or consult one online.

11.27. The best writing tip I've ever encountered comes from Richard C. Wydick's article "Plain English for Lawyers," and what's so great about his advice is that you don't have to understand more than a lick of grammar to follow it. Wydick tells us that in every sentence there are two types of words: working words, generally verbs and nouns (*italicized* below), and glue words, often prepositions, whose main purpose is to hold the sentence together (they are underlined below). The first step is to identify which words are which. The following is one of his examples:

A trial by jury was requested by the defendant.

He suggests rewriting this passive sentence as:

The defendant requested a jury trial.

The key to the improvement is moving the subject *defendant* (the person who initiated the action) closer to the beginning of the sentence, which eliminates three glue words (by, was, by). If you undertake this type of analysis in your draft papers, you can rid yourself of superfluous words, which tend to grow like weeds in a garden.

11.28. Excessive words and phrases produce chubby sentences. If you have many of them, reading your writing will be like forcing your readers to walk through a mud-covered field after a heavy rain. So, take a scalpel to your text and excise any verbiage.

Actual: *Capitalist societies highlight the fact that there is inequality between individuals.*

Revised: *Capitalist societies are unequal societies.*

This revision takes us from eleven words to five, from twenty-seven syllables to sixteen. Note that we could have ended the revised sentence with *unequal*, but that might have made it a bit too concise. I also like the rhythm generated by the repetition of *societies*.

11.29. Look closely at your sentences and delete words that aren't earning their keep, that aren't contributing to the argument. The following is an example from the *New York Review of Books*, where I would have deleted six words from this sentence with no loss of meaning.

> It seems ~~both~~ strange and ~~entirely~~ appropriate, in this sense, that arguably the most famous moment of Herzog's ~~entire~~ career—the moment I ~~myself~~, as a devotee of long standing, ~~immediately~~ remember when I think about how great Werner Herzog is—occurs in a film he did not ~~himself~~ direct.

The rewritten sentence would look like this:

> It seems strange and appropriate, in this sense, that arguably the most famous moment of Herzog's career—the moment I, as a devotee of long standing, remember when I think about how great Werner Herzog is—occurs in a film he did not direct.

That's better, but this revised sentence still sounds flabby to me. The part in between the dashes doesn't seem to add much; I would toss it. If the sentiment needs to be kept, perhaps the sentence could be written something like this:

> When I think about how great Werner Herzog is, it seems strange and appropriate that arguably the most famous moment of his career occurs in a film he did not direct.

This second revision takes the original sentence from fifty words to thirty-one, while removing the two dashes and three of the four commas (these punctuation marks interrupt the flow). Students should take heart from this example. Even a writer in one of the most prestigious literary publications in the English-speaking world can be found inflating their sentences, having earned no return on their bloated word count. The task of paring our writing, making it as fat-free as possible, is a lifelong challenge for every author.

11.30. Within paragraphs, if you need to prepare the reader for a contrast, use words such as *although, but, conversely, however, in contrast, nevertheless, though,* or *yet.*

11.31. To announce a change in time, use words such as *after, before, eventually, meanwhile, previously, since, subsequently,* or *thereafter.*

11.32. To demonstrate a cause-and-effect relationship, use *as a result, because, consequently, hence,* or *therefore.*

11.33. It's not required, but you should generally signal that you are about to introduce an example with words like *for example, for instance, in particular,* or *specifically.*

11.34. Collective nouns such as *society, capitalism,* and *the state* take the pronoun *it,* not *they.*

No: *The society faltered as a result. They later recovered by…*
Yes: *The society faltered as a result. It later recovered by…*

11.35. Especially in a paper under ten pages, avoid referring back to matters you have already discussed. Our short-term memories aren't that short. There's usually no need to have expressions like the following:

As we saw previously…

As noted in the introduction…

As discussed in the previous section…

11.36. Read drafts out loud to capture errors. When you are in the final stages of revision, your ears are often a better guide than your eyes.

PARAGRAPHS AND SENTENCES

11.37. You might receive a comment to the effect that your paper has a number of problems which make your argument difficult to follow. You may have paragraphs that are not linked, sentences within paragraphs that are not connected, sentences that are incomplete, and a number of confusing phrases, missing words, and words that are used incorrectly. In such cases, you will likely be advised to contact a staff member (perhaps in a Writing Centre) who can work with you to help you improve your writing.

11.38. Pay attention to writing trends over your career. You never want to find yourself thirty or forty years out of date. I still occasionally see professional writers using old-fashioned words like *mankind*. Be aware that if you use superseded language, you will not be regarded as an eloquent, bow-tie-wearing conservative. Rather, you will gain notoriety as an out-of-touch fuddy-duddy. And that's a moniker you don't want anyone engraving on your tombstone.

11.39. A recent controversy on language concerns personal pronouns, which replace nouns. In these instances, the individual(s) has been introduced to us; they have been named, and you are going to continue talking about them while using a substitute name (a pronoun). In applicable cases, avoid using *he or she*, *he/she*, or the hideous *s/he*, and especially avoid the sexist *he*, if this *he* is trying to stand in for all human beings. I recommend instead that you make use of *they*.

So, what about *they*, which is at the centre of our most recent pronoun dustup? Well, the jury of English-language users has returned its verdict (as has the 18th edition of *The Chicago Manual of Style*; see sec. 5.52). Yes, you can use *they* as a singular pronoun for a specific person who is nonbinary, who doesn't identify as male or female, just as we have long used it for a nonspecific person whose gender is unknown. (*They stole my bike this morning.*) So the verb *be*, to give one example, is now conjugated in the present tense as follows: For the singular, it's *I am, you are, he is, she is, they are*; and for the plural, it's *we are, you are, they are*. For a few hundred years, beginning slowly around Shakespeare's time, we have used the same pronoun (*you*) and the same verb (*are*) for both the singular and the plural (with *you are* replacing *thou art* in the singular). And yet, no one today seems confused by this use nor are they particularly agitated by it. In sum, *you* has been genderless in the singular and the plural forms for centuries, so why can't *they* be? Keep in mind, too, that expressions such as "the men and women of the third division" should now be considered exclusionary. You can store them in a file with the title *Extinct English*, where they will sit alongside *thee, forsooth, poetess* and other such anachronisms.

FURTHER READING

My template paragraph, with the topic sentence as your first sentence, is useful as a basic model which you can employ almost continuously, especially if you feel your writing rests on shaky ground. Over time, however, you should cultivate a more creative style, where paragraphs don't always follow the same organizing principle. For the best work on the subject, see Bruce Ross-Larson's short book *Powerful Paragraphs*, where he covers nineteen ways to make your key point (including in the middle or at the end of a paragraph) and thirteen ways to link paragraphs, with examples for all his suggestions. This book, along with two other Ross-Larson works (*Stunning Sentences* and *Riveting Reports*), has been published as a single volume, *Effective Writing*. It doesn't hurt to own the three-in-one version, but the crucial book to have is the one on paragraphs.

For improving your work at the sentence level, see Richard C. Wydick's "Plain English for Lawyers." This article was eventually published as part of a book with the same name, though its expansion mostly involved adding some instructions on punctuation. The heart of Wydick's approach can be found in the article, a PDF of which is available on Google Scholar.

See also June Casagrande's *It Was the Best of Sentences, It Was the Worst of Sentences*. In twenty-one brief chapters—with titles such as "Size Matters: Short Versus Long Sentences" and "To Know Them Is to Hating Them: Faulty and Funky Parallels"—Casagrande provides a great series of suggestions on how to craft lucid sentences.

Take a look as well at Brandon Royal's *The Little Red Writing Book*, with its twenty short chapters, each of which highlights a principle of good writing, including "employ the six basic writing structures," "favor verbs, not nouns," and "use transition words."

I'm also a huge fan of Helen Sword's *The Writer's Diet*, which is a mere seventy-seven pages. In five slim chapters, she gives readers guidance for dealing quickly with a number of writing issues, such as avoiding noun density, trimming "prepositional podge," and rolling back the use of "waste words."

For more writing tips see William Strunk Jr. and E. B. White's *The Elements of Style*, which is still valuable, though a few of its "rules" are outdated, so you should read it alongside some of the other books I recommend here.

To take your sentences to a higher level, review the great tips in Jack Hart's *Wordcraft*. This book is aimed at journalists, but it has plenty of sound advice for students and academics. His chapters on structure, force, brevity, rhythm, and voice are especially good. The first edition of *Wordcraft* was published by Anchor in 2007 as *A Writer's Coach*. Either edition is fine.

You should also add Brooks Landon's *Building Great Sentences* to your "higher level" reading list. Its fifteen chapters include "The Rhythm of Cumulative Syntax," "The Riddle of Prose Rhythm," "Suspensive Syntax: The Rhythm of Delay," and "The Rhythm of

Threes." The summary on the book's cover says it "celebrates the sheer joy of language—and will forever change the way you read and write." I agree with this assessment.

And pick up a copy of Mark Forsyth's *The Elements of Eloquence*. His twenty-nine short chapters focus on rhetoric, "the techniques for making a single phrase striking and memorable just by altering the wording." You are likely familiar with some of these techniques, such as alliteration, hyperbole, and rhetorical questioning. But Forsyth will introduce you to dozens more, including polysyndeton (repeating conjunctions—*I ran and I fell and I bled.*) and anadiplosis (repeating the last word or two of a clause or sentence as the first word or two of what follows—*To die, to sleep—To sleep, perchance to dream.*). You don't have to memorize the names of these techniques; indeed, they are instantly forgettable. You just need to be able to recognize them when you see them and to use them judiciously in your own work.

For editing, the best book by far is Joseph M. Williams's *Style*. Written for an academic audience, I know of no other book that so skillfully teaches writers to diagnose problems and then edit sentences to maximize, as the book's subtitle puts it, the "clarity and grace" of their prose. The most recent edition is the thirteenth, published in 2021 by Pearson Education with co-author Joseph Bizup. This edition seems to be available as an ebook only. The subtitle of *Style* was *Ten Lessons in Clarity and Grace* until the eighth edition. At that point, it became *Lessons in Clarity and Grace*, with the addition of a few chapters, which mostly serve to fatten the book, superimposing some middle-aged flab on top of what once was a solid six-pack. *Style* is expensive, and it's not easy to find reasonably priced secondhand copies. I own the ninth edition, but I'd say any one from the fourth edition onward will serve you well. I recommend purchasing the most recently published one that you can afford.

I also like Bruce Ross-Larson's *Edit Yourself*, with its eleven short chapters (totaling forty-two pages), plus another sixty or so pages where he has "arranged, in alphabetical order, more than 1,500 common cuts, changes, and comparisons that editors make to produce clear, concise writing."

For a recent, wonderful addition to the literature, see Pamela Haag's *Revise*. Her thirteen chapters contain ninety pieces of advice, each of which is roughly one to five pages. Some examples include "data dumping," "throat-clearing, or warm-up prose," "identify your go-to punctuation crutch and revise it," and "replace stilted prose with natural language."

Finally, for the most helpful guide to bias-free language, see the APA's *Publication Manual* (chapter 5, pp. 131–49). See also *The Chicago Manual of Style*, sec. 5.255 to 5.266, for information on "Inclusive Language and Minimizing Bias."

12. Punctuation

If you constantly misuse punctuation, you will make it challenging for someone to read your paper and follow your ideas. Mastering the mechanics of punctuation will help you improve your writing immensely and so get your message across to your instructors. This chapter covers typical usages for three punctuation marks: commas, semicolons, and apostrophes.

COMMAS: SEVEN USES

The comma is the most frequently used punctuation mark, so it is essential to learn how to employ it flawlessly. Its misuse will force a reader to constantly move back and forth in an effort to understand your meaning. After a while, this reader will become so obsessed with mentally correcting your endless comma gaffes, they will no longer hear your voice, no longer hear the argument you are making. The misused commas, and the commas that never appeared where they should have, will be like little pin pricks hammering away at the reader's brain, draining their energy and dissipating their attention.

There are dozens of occasions when you need to use commas. The following seven are probably the most common ones:

12.1. To connect what could stand as two complete sentences, each with a subject and a verb. They are separated by a comma and a conjunction such as *and*, *but*, *so*, *then*, or *yet*.

He ate a sandwich drowning in mayonnaise, then he vomited shortly thereafter.

In this type of sentence, the comma is optional if at least one half of the sentence is relatively short.

Yes: *I tripped, then I fell.*
Yes: *I tripped then I fell.*
Yes: *I tripped, then I fell and hit my head.*
Yes: *I tripped then I fell and hit my head.*

12.2. After an introductory phrase, which usually precedes the subject and the verb.

With that track record, I knew he was going to lose.
On second thought, I agreed she shouldn't go.

For clarity, I strongly recommend you use this comma, except if the phrase is extremely brief. In these instances, you can use it or omit it.

Yes: *On Monday, I'm leaving for Paris.*
Yes: *On Monday I'm leaving for Paris.*

12.3. When a sentence begins with a dependent clause followed by an independent clause.

If he could walk to the store on his own, I wouldn't have to get out of my pyjamas.

The dependent clause has the subject *he* and the verbal clause *could walk*, but it loses its independence because of that little conjunction *if*, which doesn't allow the clause to stand as a sentence.

12.4. Before *and* after words, phrases, or clauses that are not required to understand the meaning of the sentence.

The man on the corner, with a hockey helmet on his head, proceeded to jaywalk across the street.

You will know you've done this correctly if you can remove the phrase and you still have a complete and comprehensible sentence.

The man on the corner proceeded to jaywalk across the street.

The use of this comma entails a judgement call. If someone were testifying in court, after reviewing a photograph of a group of men standing on the corner, the *with a hockey helmet on his head* might be necessary if we are to understand who did what.

Meanwhile, essential words, phrases, or clauses must *not* be set off with commas.

Jacob's sister Arlene just left for university.

In this case, we can assume that *Arlene* is essential because Jacob must have at least one other sister, and that's why we need to know Arlene's name.

12.5. To separate a series of items in a list.

He put lettuce, tomatoes, and onions on his burger.

For clarity, you should always use a comma before the final item in a series, like the one that comes after *tomatoes* and before *and* in the example above. If you are not convinced by that advice, know that this "Oxford comma" is required by three of the most important style guides: Chicago, MLA, and APA.

12.6. When you precede a quotation with words such as *concluded, noted,* or *argued*.

He concluded, "I'm not sure how this happened."

You do not need a comma if the quotation has been integrated into the sentence (often with the assistance of a word like *that*).

She maintained that it was "a clear crime against humanity."

You do not need a comma (or quotation marks) when you are indirectly quoting, when you are summarizing in your own words what someone said or wrote.

They told me to take the money and run.

12.7. To replace parentheses, which are rather intrusive, and so hard on the eyes. One of the last tasks I undertake with any manuscript is to see if parentheses can be removed and replaced by commas—or perhaps dashes. They often can be.

Ok: *Fred Smith (the younger brother of George Smith) won the award.*

Better: *Fred Smith, the younger brother of George Smith, won the award.*

You can also consider deleting the parenthetical information or rewriting the sentence to avoid parentheses *or* commas.

In sum, don't put commas where they are not required and be sure to put them where they are. That means learning the rules for their placement. If you find these rules difficult to master, you can proceed by reading your writing out loud. At the places where you pause naturally and feel yourself taking a short breath, you likely need a comma. If you have to guess, this is a decent method to use, though it's not close to being flawless.

SEMICOLONS: THREE USES

In my experience, few students make extensive use of semicolons, and those who do often use them incorrectly. The good news, though, is that you can ignore them. So, either dispense with them entirely or learn to employ them correctly. Semicolons are used as follows:

12.8. To connect what could stand as two complete sentences, each with a subject and a verb. A semicolon can be used when the second thought seems to rapidly follow the first one.

> *He ate a sandwich drowning in <u>mayonnaise; he</u> vomited shortly thereafter.*

In this instance, you can avoid the semicolon by using a conjunction and a comma instead.

> *He ate a sandwich drowning in <u>mayonnaise, then he</u> vomited shortly thereafter.*

12.9. To connect two sentences with a conjunctive adverb in the middle, such as *however, nevertheless,* or *therefore*. In this case, use the formula [semicolon] + [word] + [comma].

> *Smith said she was out of her <u>league; however, others</u> disagreed with his view.*

This is another instance where you can avoid the semicolon by using a conjunction and a comma instead.

> *Smith said she was out of her <u>league, but others</u> disagreed with his view.*

12.10. To separate long lists, when there would be too many commas if there were no semicolons.

We visited Louisdale, Nova Scotia; Fredericton, New Brunswick; North Bay, Ontario; and Victoria, British Columbia.

In this case, you can avoid semicolons by avoiding long lists. You can spread the details throughout a number of sentences or you can rewrite the sentence, foregoing the need for excessive detail.

We visited Nova Scotia, New Brunswick, Ontario, and British Columbia.

APOSTROPHES: THREE USES

The first thing you should know about apostrophes is that they are never used to change a word from the singular to the plural. *Never.* This includes abbreviations and years, so that, for example, it's one BMW but two or more BMWs, and the 1990s, not the 1990's. Apostrophes are used as follows:

12.11. To indicate possession.

John's car
the dog's food (one dog)
the dogs' food (two or more dogs)
an angel's wings
the girls' treehouse
the children's toys

If a person's name ends in *s*, you should add an *s* after the apostrophe.

Charles's crown

The idea of possession or ownership is also applied to certain expressions ("quasi-possessives"). These uses can be difficult to discern, so listen closely to what your ear is telling you.

all in a day's work

the shed's roof

one week's vacation

two weeks' vacation

the war's consequences (one war)

the wars' consequences (two or more wars)

Note that in the following example the singular *pansy* has become the plural *pansies* (without the use of an apostrophe!). The apostrophe is then added to show that these pansies "own" something—their colours.

The pansies' colours give these flowers a cheerful look.

Don't beat yourself up if you get a possessive wrong every now and then. I recently read (in a book published by a major university press, no less) about "the Peasant's War of 1524–25." On discovering this, I felt sorry for the poor fella who had to double as a one-man army, though it seems that, given those dates, he managed to hold off the enemy for more than a year. (Rumour has it he was so proud he gave himself a medal.)

12.12. To create contractions, typically when two words are rolled into one. The apostrophe stands in for the omitted letters.

I am = I'm

I would = I'd

I cannot = I can't

I will not = I won't

you will = you'll

you were not = you weren't
he has gone = he's gone
it does not = it doesn't
we will not = we won't
they are = they're

Note that contractions are not used much in formal writing. But you can employ them infrequently, especially if you feel they improve the rhythm of a sentence. Also, there will be times when formal just seems *too* formal.

Ok: *Let us imagine a scenario where...*

Better: *Let's imagine a scenario where...*

12.13. They are rarely needed, but apostrophes are used to indicate the plural of letters.

Polish surnames seem to have a lot of y's and z's.

If we omitted the apostrophes in this case, the sentence would look like it contains a couple of typos.

Polish surnames seem to have a lot of ys and zs.

FURTHER READING

For the essential guide, purchase a copy of June Casagrande's *The Best Punctuation Book, Period*. (It truly is.) You can refer to this work to answer all your punctuation questions. In addition to the three marks noted in this chapter, she gives thorough coverage of the period, the colon, quotation marks, the question mark, the exclamation point, ellipses, the hyphen, parentheses and brackets, the slash and backslash—and the em-dash and en-dash (who knew?). Part 2 ("Punctuation A to Z"), pp. 149–232, is a glossary of common terms and abbreviations, indicating how each of them is punctuated by four style guides (Chicago, APA, MLA, and the *Associated Press Stylebook*). It answers questions such as: Do you use in-depth or in depth? US or U.S.? Windchill or wind chill?

The Chicago Manual of Style can always be counted on for great advice, including its coverage of the forty or so reasons to use a comma; see chapter 6 ("Punctuation"), pp. 377–440.

For a more targeted survey, see chapter 3 (pp. 20–66) of *Dreyer's English*, by Benjamin Dreyer, in which he covers, from his perspective as an editor, "the punctuational issues/problems/knots/dilemmas I've most encountered."

See also Lynne Truss's *Eats, Shoots, and Leaves*, an informative and humorous bestseller that has sold over three million copies. Some writers find her marching orders a bit heavy-handed, but in a world overrun with errant apostrophes and misused quotation marks, I admit to having a soft spot for her take-no-prisoners approach, especially her admonition, "don't use commas like a stupid person."

And once you have mastered the mechanics of punctuation, take a look at Noah Lukeman's *The Art of Punctuation*, which, as its title suggests, focuses on how you can use commas, colons, dashes, and the like to take your writing to a higher level—how to use and underuse each mark, the dangers of overuse and underuse, and what your preference for certain marks "reveals about you." After reading his book, you will see punctuation from a new perspective—and I guarantee you will never be able to go back to your wide-eyed, innocent way of approaching these funny little scratch marks. (By the way, did you notice those recent, artful dashes?)

13. Quotations

Knowing what to quote, what to paraphrase or summarize, and what to ignore is one of the litmus tests that separate strong papers from weak ones. As a general rule, try to minimize direct quotation. By putting ideas in your own words, you show that you have thought about the issues and that you understand what is being said. If you quote too much, you will fade into the background. You will be left with a work full of quotations, an interminable collection of other people's voices.

There are three good reasons to quote as opposed to summarizing or paraphrasing: (1) you cannot think of a better way of expressing the thought. The author's words are "right on," in particular because they have used a distinct or apt phrase; (2) you are analyzing a complex passage in detail, hence it is necessary to quote it so the reader can follow along; and (3) when a reader may be skeptical of a claim you are making if you put it in your own words, so you quote to show you are not misrepresenting another person's views.

TIPS FOR EFFECTIVE QUOTING

13.1. Do not have a paper with no quotations (unless instructed to). This will lead a reader to wonder why you could not find anything worth quoting from your research. Always squeeze a few small quotations into your text to demonstrate that you have an eye for thoughtful, innovative phrases and that you know how to incorporate them into an argument. For a five-page paper, I recommend having four to eight short quotations of five to twenty-five words each. That is, have some quotes but not too many.

13.2. Avoid resorting to long, extended quotations (of around forty or more words). They take up valuable space that you should be reluctant to concede to someone else. A short paper of five or six pages should probably have none of these quotations. In a longer paper (say twenty pages) you might want to have two or three at most. Having none is best. Try to reduce a long quotation down to one or two short snippets. Look for the evocative phrase in the lengthy passage that attracted you to it in the first place. Even then, on revision, you should ask of all your quotations, long or short: Do I need this specific language? Or can I put it in my own words (and still cite it, of course)?

13.3. Do not quote boring information, including statistics that you can easily paraphrase in your own words (with a citation, if necessary). Given that you will have only a few quotations, they should not entail adding listless language to your paper. Make sure they are insightful, pithy, and beautifully written.

13.4. Do not have a quotation as a topic sentence—the first sentence of a paragraph. The entry way into each of your mini-arguments should be in your own words. Your voice makes clear that you are the one directing the argument; you are the one in charge. Quotations are generally other people's words that support the point you have made in your topic sentence or they are words with which you will take issue. With that in mind, you also should not have a quotation in a paragraph's concluding sentence, when you are wrapping up.

13.5. Avoid quoting complete sentences. If you do this often, it suggests you might not be integrating ideas into your argument, into your own sentences.

13.6. Do not shoehorn a quotation into your text, one that is not precisely related to the point you are trying to make. Shoehorned quotations don't form part of a discussion. They just sit on the page, like an old dog snoozing in the sun, its tongue flopping out. This use of quotations is a lame attempt to add credence to a weak argument, and it will be obvious to whoever grades your paper. Your quotations must be there for a reason.

THE MECHANICS OF QUOTING

13.7. In the leadup to a quotation (or a citation of any kind), you don't need to mention the title of your source, and you can probably leave out the author's name as well (or keep only their surname). These are distracting words that add little.

Ok: *In* Fired up About Capitalism, *Tom Malleson (2016, 114) suggests that the "issue today is a struggle over what powerful people desire versus what regular people are organized enough to demand."*

Better: *Malleson (2016, 114) suggests that the "issue today is a struggle over what powerful people desire versus what regular people are organized enough to demand."*

Best: *It is likely the case that the "issue today is a struggle over what powerful people desire versus what regular people are organized enough to demand" (Malleson 2016, 114).*

The difference between these three acceptable practices is that for the "best" sentence, a reader, whether reading out loud or in their head, will skip over the citation, whereas in the "better" example they will read "Malleson" and in the "ok" example they will read, "In *Fired up About Capitalism*, Tom Malleson." The "ok" example gives us too many needless words. And while the "better" example gives us just a single extra word ("Malleson"), if you use this style of attribution throughout the paper, you will end up with a lot of phrases like "Malleson suggests…," "Dunbar-Ortiz asserts…," "Gilio-Whitaker maintains…," and so on. This can get irritating rather quickly. And the constant "calling out" of sources also places a crimp on your effort to develop a more literary style.

Meanwhile, the "best" approach avoids disrupting the flow of the text by pushing the reference to the end of a sentence, or sometimes before a comma in mid-sentence, or to a footnote or endnote. In sum, as much as possible, try to integrate the citations for your quotations silently, so they remain muted, off in the background. You are obligated to give credit to other writers for their words and ideas. You are not required to shout that credit from the rooftops. Still, in some disciplines, you may be expected to mention the author's surname in the leadup to a quotation. Be aware of what the expectations are between disciplines. You can figure this out by noticing how surnames are handled in your course readings.

13.8. You may feel the need to mention an author from time to time, usually if you are in direct discussion with them or you want to emphasize their groundbreaking contribution to a debate. In such cases, an effective way of quoting would be something like:

[surname] + [verb] + *that* + [the quotation]

Malleson maintains that "activist organizations must be microcosms of the world that we wish to live in" (131).

Other useful verbs to use in this situation include *argue, assert, claim, contend, demonstrate, note, observe, propose*, and *suggest*. Avoid *state* and also avoid *say*, unless perhaps you are reciting a memory or quoting the words of someone you interviewed.

No: *Malleson says the "issue today…*

Yes: *My grandmother said, "I remember it well."*

And never use that journalistic travesty *opine*.

No, no, no: *Patriquin opines that some words are so ugly, they need to be buried in the backyard, preferably near a pine tree to mask the smell.*

13.9. If you mention the author in the leadup to a quotation, don't mention them again immediately following. And don't draw attention to a quotation using the word *quote*.

This quote by Malleson…
As the quote asserts…
This quote shows that…

13.10. A comma is typically used after *noted, argued*, and similar verbs when introducing a quotation.

Garratt argues, "We believe that…

13.11. A colon can be used rather than a comma for emphasis.

Wilkinson testified: "It's my understanding…

13.12. When a quotation is introduced by a complete sentence, a colon should be used.

Mary Anderson defines it as follows: "An author is…

13.13. Place a colon or a semicolon after a quotation mark.

Smith (2007, 12) said she was "out of her league"; however, others disagreed with his view.

13.14. In North America, a period or a comma comes before a closing quotation mark. A citation number appears after that quotation mark. There is no space between the number and the punctuation, be it a quotation mark, a period, or a comma, so make sure they all snuggle up close.

She said she was "tired of life and all its pain."[5]

In the UK, the citation number would appear after the final period, as in ... *pain*'.[5]

13.15. Block quotations are handled differently. They also have different minimum requirements depending on the style guide in use. For MLA, they consist of more than four lines of text; for APA, they are forty or more words; and for Chicago, they are (usually) more than one hundred words. When you want to quote something this lengthy, you block it off from the rest of the text by indenting it about one inch from the left margin. Do not add quotation marks; the indenting is enough to alert the reader that you are quoting. And you probably won't offend anyone if you follow Chicago's advice to left-justify (back to the margin) the first sentence of the paragraph that comes after a block quote, if you are planning to discuss its significance. If you took care of that task before the quotation, you can indent and start a new paragraph.

13.16. Quote verbatim (word-for-word). You quote a passage *exactly* as you see it on the page. If words are italicized, you italicize them. If words within the quotation are themselves in quotation marks, you keep those marks. With rare exceptions, do not alter anything without informing the reader that you have done so.

13.17. If you omit words from a direct quotation, indicate that you have done this by using an ellipsis (...), which consists of three dots with a space on either side. You may want to drop some of the author's words when they are unimportant (such as "which we saw in the previous chapter") or because they do not fit the grammatical structure of your sentence.

> *Today, we "are told that these ideas are old-fashioned...and must be discarded" (Kerry, 2010, p. 10).*

Do not use the ellipsis to join a variety of phrases, scattered across a page or two. If you do, you might misrepresent the views of the author.

13.18. Do not place an ellipsis before or after a quotation. It is understood when you have a quotation that you have left out everything that appeared in the text before the quoted words and everything that followed them, so there's no need to emphasize that fact.

> **No:** *She said she was "...broken by the struggle" and so removed herself from the battle.*[5]
>
> **Yes:** *She said she was "broken by the struggle" and so removed herself from the battle.*[5]

13.19. Use brackets when you want to add a word or phrase to a quotation. This is usually done to make the quotation fit the grammatical structure of your sentence or to clarify something that may be unclear to the reader.

> *According to Carter, when "we first meet him [Hamlet], a...."*

Don't overuse brackets. You can often dispense with them (and the use of ellipses) by trimming words out of the beginning or the ending of a proposed quotation, by interspersing your own words with a few brief quotations, or by rearranging your sentence. In addition, avoid cumbersome interjections simply by changing the place where the quotation starts. The following example involves quoting a sentence that begins, "The report had its origins in...."

No: *She claimed that "[t]he report had its origins in...."*

Yes: *She claimed that the "report had its origins in...."*

Having said that, you could simply begin the quote "*the report had...*" without acknowledging you surreptitiously changed a capital *T* to a small one (which Chicago style says you are free to do). But given the ubiquity of these opening brackets, I suspect some academics fear that such a craven act of deception might turn the scholarly ship on its side, a fatal blow to its civilizing mission, drowning it in a snotgreen sea (apologies to James Joyce).

13.20. Do not begin a quotation with information in brackets. (I see academics doing this all the time. It drives me bonkers.)

No: *Malleson notes that "[today there] is a struggle over what powerful people desire versus what regular people are organized enough to demand."[2]*

Yes: *Malleson notes that today there "is a struggle over what powerful people desire versus what regular people are organized enough to demand."[2]*

13.21. You may want to italicize a word in the quotation for emphasis, a word that is not italicized in the original (such as *not* in the following example). If you do, indicate that you have done so by using a phrase such as "emphasis added" somewhere in your reference.

Thomas (1999, p. 68, emphasis added) argued that "capitalism did not *exist anywhere at this time."*

If you quote a phrase with emphasis placed in the original text by the author, the reader should understand that it was the author's doing. As a result, you shouldn't need to add a redundant "emphasis in original."

13.22. In a quotation with a technical or grammatical error, you can use the italicized word *sic* in brackets, which tells the reader, "This mistake is not mine; it was in the original."

> Konrad was adamant that "elements of the story didn't jive [sic] with her understanding of the matter."[8]

You can avoid using *sic* in the same ways that you can avoid using ellipses and brackets. You especially don't want to use this device to deliver a gloating "gotcha," bragging to the world that you found a misused word or an unfortunate typo in some famous author's work. Stuff happens.

13.23. If there is a quotation within the phrase or sentence you wish to quote, distinguish it from your own by using double quotation marks and single quotation marks. If you are in North America, use "doubles" for the overall quote and 'singles' for the quote within the overall quote.

> The Senate report (Canada 1970, 3) notes that "the majority of the poor have difficulty accessing the 'good life' because they have little money."

In this instance, you are quoting the Senate report *and* the Senate report quoting the "good life" phrase.

If you are in the UK, you would format the sentence like this:

> The Senate report (Canada 1970, 3) notes that 'the majority of the poor have difficulty accessing the "good life" because they have little money'.

Also, if single and double quotation marks appear one right after the other, you can separate them with a space or leave them alone to snuggle up close.

13.24. Be careful to whom you attribute ideas. Do not claim to be quoting, say, Joe Smith if you are quoting a section of the Senate report found in Joe Smith's book. And when you quote a passage which in turn has been quoted by another scholar (and so you have not read the passage in the original source), tell us that you found it "quoted in" so-and-so's work. This gives credit to the person who discovered this information and brought it to your attention.

> *The* Senate Report on Poverty *(quoted in Smith 1993, 52) concludes that "the majority of the poor…*

This way, too, you do not give the impression that you have read the original. For example, if you have Karl Marx's *Capital* in your bibliography, the assumption will be that you have, in fact, read this work of 800+ pages. It is perfectly acceptable to say you found Marx's words in Joe Smith's book (or wherever).

I have seen at least one writing guide for students suggest that you should always cite the original source as well as the source where you found the quotation, so you can confirm that the words were reproduced accurately. I disagree. That's time consuming, and I'm not sure it's necessary. We have to trust other scholars to do their work properly. If we can't depend on them to copy a quotation correctly, how can we trust them on more important matters, such as their argument and their evidence?

13.25. Quotation marks are also used for "scare quotes." You can use these marks when you want to make clear that you are employing a word ironically. That is, you are not using it in its ordinary meaning, but rather in the opposite of that meaning.

> *The dictator bragged about his people's "freedom."*

The author here is suggesting that that *freedom* should be understood as "lack of freedom." Be frugal with your use of scare quotes. Too many might suggest you didn't want to bother searching for the precise words you should have used. Also, you can avoid scare quotes by employing *so-called* instead.

The dictator bragged about his people's so-called freedom.

13.26. When you have the next-to-final draft of your paper prepared, check all quotations for accuracy. Have each of your sources on paper or onscreen, then compare them word-for-word with what you typed onto the page. Based on what I've noticed reviewing quotations in my own drafts, I can guarantee you will be appalled by how many mistakes you find.

FURTHER READING

On the mechanics of quoting, see *MLA Handbook*, sec. 6.31 to 6.68, pp. 252–80; and *The Chicago Manual of Style*, chapter 12 ("Quotations and Dialogue"), pp. 731–71.

14. Words to Watch

In your drafts, you will find plenty of words that should make you pause, where a little voice in your head asks, "Is *that* correct?" This chapter includes the words that students often stumble over, for example writing *then* where *than* is required. Learn to recognize the words that give you problems, and keep an eye out for them.

14.1. its / it's

When it comes to words that get mixed up, this pair is the undisputed champion:

Its indicates possession.
It's is a contraction of *it is* or *it has*.

The cat licked its paw.
It's [It is] a sunny day.
It's [It has] been a long time.

These are almost certainly the most commonly confused words in the English language. This is because we typically use an apostrophe when indicating possession—for example, *Tom's car is red*—but we do not with *its*. There is an easy way to avoid this error. Whenever you see *it's*, you should be able to insert the phrase *it is* or *it has*. For example: *The cat licked it's paw* would be read as *The cat licked it is paw*. That's clearly wrong, so you can delete the apostrophe. Note that *its'* (with an apostrophe at the end) is never used.

The following are all runners-up, presented in alphabetical order.

14.2. accept / except
Accept means to receive something or believe something.
Except means "other than."

The actor will accept the award with pride.

He must accept his fate.

Everyone except John is going to university.

14.3. adapt / adopt
Adapt means to modify behaviour to suit new conditions.
Adopt means to take up an idea or follow a course of action.

The Russians were forced to adapt to a capitalist economy.

The government chose to adopt a controversial position on the issue.

14.4. affect / effect (verbs)
Affect means "to influence."
Effect means "to bring about."

Did the vaccination policy affect his decision to quit?

The aim of revolution is to effect fundamental change.

14.5. affect / effect (nouns)
Affect refers to feeling or emotion. (This word is used mainly by psychologists.)

Effect refers to an outcome.

The patient displayed a lack of affect.

The effect of such a loss can be devastating.

14.6. conscience / conscious

Conscience is a noun that refers to moral principles of right and wrong.

Conscious is an adjective that refers to an awareness of something.

If you have any conscience, you will not steal that jacket.

She was not conscious of the fact that her husband was a mass murderer.

14.7. fewer / less

Fewer usually refers to items that can be counted.

Less usually refers to general amounts that are not easily counted.

She owns fewer books than he does.

He has less energy than he did before.

This distinction can get tricky, because you should use *less* with, among others, time, distance, weight, and money, which we can count. If you listen to your ear, though, you should get it right almost every time.

14.8. lead / led

Lead (pronounced *led*) is a metal.
Lead (pronounced *leed*) is a verb meaning "to guide."
Led is the past tense of the verb "to lead."

The fish contained lead.

You can lead a horse to water, but you cannot make it drink.

She led the horse to water yesterday, but it still wouldn't drink.

14.9. loose / lose

Loose means "not secure."
Lose refers to a defeat or when something has been misplaced.

The top button on my shirt is loose.

You should learn how to lose graciously.

Did you lose your car keys?

14.10. passed / past

Passed is the past tense of "to pass."
Past means "belonging to a former time" or "beyond a place."

She passed the exam.

It's all in the past.

The liquor store is past the next intersection.

14.11. principal / principle

A *principal* is an individual who is the head of a school. The word can also mean "most important" or an amount of money that has been borrowed.
Principle refers to basic moral beliefs or rules.

The school children were afraid of the principal.

The principal problem with today's youth is that they don't have enough grit.

The interest rate on his mortgage was so high he had difficulty paying down the principal.

The principle "thou shalt not kill" is part of every culture.

14.12. quash / squash

Quash means to suppress something (often forcibly) or reverse a legal decision.
Squash means to crush something, to flatten it.

The police quashed the rebellion.

The Appeals Court quashed his conviction.

She squashed the spider with her big toe.

14.13. than / then
Than is used to compare.
Then means "at that time" or "soon afterward."

I am taller than my father.

Back then, life was easier.

Let's eat first, then we'll go to the mall.

14.14. that / which
That is used with an essential (or "defining") clause or phrase, which is not set off by commas.

Which is usually used with a nonessential (or "commenting") clause or phrase, which *is* set off by commas.

The car <u>that I drive</u> is ready for the junk yard.

My car, <u>which is twenty years old</u>, is ready for the junk yard.

In the *that* sentence, the underlined part is essential to the meaning of the sentence, letting us know which specific car is ready for the junk yard. In contrast, the *which* phrase can be dropped from the sentence so that it reads, *My car is ready for the junkyard*. Note also that the distinction between *that* and *which* can be a question of style and not a question of grammar. For instance, some guides suggest both *which* and *that* would be acceptable in our *that* sentence, so you could have, *The car <u>which I drive</u> is ready for the junk yard*. In contrast, our *which* sentence (with the twenty-year old car) requires a *which*. In a student paper, you can usually follow your ear on whether to use *that* or *which* (as opposed to preparing a work for publication, where you would follow the publisher's style guide).

14.15. that / which / who

That and *which* refer to things.
Who refers to persons, or to animals with names.

She picked up the flowers that fell off the table.

These rights, which are guaranteed by law, make democracy work.

They are the men who robbed the bank.

Wren is the kind of dog who loves to wag her tail.

14.16. their / there / they're

Their is the possessive of *they*.
There refers to a place.
They're is a contraction of *they are*.

We were driving their new truck.

We're going over there this afternoon.

They're crazy.

14.17. who / whom

I have difficulty understanding the distinction between *who* and *whom*, so I won't even attempt to explain it. Let's just go with the following, from the *Paperback Oxford English Dictionary* (OED):

Who, a pronoun, is used as the subject of a verb.

Whom, a pronoun, is used instead of *who* as the object of a verb or a preposition.

Who decided this?

Whom do you think we should support?

The OED adds that "when speaking, however, most people think it's acceptable to use *who* instead of *whom*, as in, *Who do you think we should support?*" According to some experts, *whom* can almost be ignored in writing as well because it has been slowly disappearing from the language (though these experts have been making this claim for at least a hundred years). Still, *whom* has its advocates. For instance, Bill Bryson finds "a certain elegance in seeing a tricky *whom* properly applied," though he also admits that "preserving the distinction between *who* and *whom* does nothing to promote clarity or reduce ambiguity." Furthermore, when *whom* is used, it is frequently used incorrectly, in a misguided attempt to sound posh. I also suspect that you are much more likely to find *who* in a written text than *whom*. Given all this, if you have to guess at which word to use, go with *who*. The one exception would be near the beginning of a sentence, when *whom* should appear after a preposition such as *with* or *to*.

With whom are you staying?

To whom did you give the book?

That still leaves us with the *whoever/whomever* conundrum. Fortunately, Bryan A. Garner (in *The Chicago Manual of Style*) has come up with a solution: Simply ignore these words and substitute *anyone who* or *anyone* instead.

Yes: *Give this book to <u>whoever</u> wants it.*

Yes: *Give this book to <u>anyone who</u> wants it.*

Yes: *I cook for <u>whomever</u> I love.*

Yes: *I cook for <u>anyone</u> I love.*

His proposed solution is easy to implement because almost everyone knows they should not write the following sentences:

No: *Give this book to <u>anyone</u> wants it.*

No: *I cook for <u>anyone whom</u> I love.*

14.18. who's / whose
Who's is a contraction of *who is* or *who has*.
Whose indicates possession.

Who's [Who is] there?
Who's [Who has] seen the movie?
Whose laptop is on the floor?

14.19. you're / your
You're is a contraction of *you are*.
Your is a possessive adjective that means "belonging to you."

You're [You are] never on time!
Your sweater is on backwards.

This distinction is easy to discern, yet for some reason I tend to mix up these words when I'm writing, so I've gotten into the habit of giving them a second (and third) look every time I see one on a page.

That's a quick overview of some of the most commonly confused words. Take note of the ones you tend to foul up or at least need to double-check. My "watch list" includes *alternative/alternate, comprise/compose, further/farther, historic/historical, home/hone, infer/imply, insidious/invidious, loath/loathe*—and, to my everlasting shame, *who/whom*. I should add as well that when a *lay* or a *lie* finds itself hanging on the tip of my pen, I run screaming in the opposite direction. In these instances, I remind myself that just about every word in the English language has at least one synonym (*lay* = put, place, deposit; *lie* = recline, rest).

FURTHER READING

See *Bryson's Dictionary of Troublesome Words*, by Bill Bryson, which is well written with a good dose of humour. He surveys words that are often confused, misused, and misspelled, like *who* and *whom* (pp. 213–15).

See also Bryan A. Garner's superb "Glossary of Problematic Words and Phrases," which is part of his "Grammar and Usage" chapter in *The Chicago Manual of Style*, sec. 5.254, pp. 318–71. It contains a short discussion of *who* and *whom* (and *whoever* and *whomever*) on p. 370.

For a briefer tour, see chapter 10 ("The Confusables") in *Dreyer's English,* by Benjamin Dreyer. This book also takes a stab at explaining *who* and *whom* (pp. 86–88).

15. Writing Dos and Don'ts

The advice in this chapter centres mostly around questions of style, not grammar. It's permissible to use unconventional style, but only if you know what the standard is, and you want to take a more daring approach because you hope to add something of value to your text. So, be aware that style often involves controversy. For example, among two of my favourite language mavens, Bill Bryson would approve of this chapter's title while Lynne Truss would insist it should have been written *Do's and Don't's* (the same style we use for *p's* and *q's*). You are free, therefore, to ignore these wonderful tips, though I suggest you follow them diligently. I cover a series of clunkers that for me are as irritating as dripping water. It would be bad enough if they appeared only in student papers, but I also spot them frequently in works by academics and journalists.

15.1. Excise *actually* from your vocabulary.

No: *It wasn't a dog; it was <u>actually</u> a wolf.*

Yes: *It wasn't a dog; it was a wolf.*

15.2. Excise *really* from your vocabulary.

No: *She <u>really</u> left him by the side of the road.*
Yes: *She left him by the side of the road.*

15.3. Excise *literally* from your vocabulary.

No: *He <u>literally</u> crashed through the window.*
Yes: *He crashed through the window.*

15.4. Excise *utterly* from your vocabulary.

No: *Harold's penchant for loud burping is <u>utterly</u> disgusting.*
Yes: *Harold's penchant for loud burping is disgusting.*

15.5. Excise *definitely* from your vocabulary.

No: *It was <u>definitely</u> the easiest way to go.*
Yes: *It was the easiest way to go.*

And should you ever have the temerity to use *definitely*, don't write it as *defiantly*.

15.6. Avoid using *very*. The word suggests you may need to employ a more effective adjective.

No: *He is <u>very cold</u>.*
Yes: *He is <u>cold</u>.*
Better: *He is <u>freezing</u>.*

15.7. Use *while* instead of *whilst*. *While* is easier to pronounce, and *whilst* sounds overly formal, even a bit pretentious.

No: *<u>Whilst</u> we were dancing…*
Yes: *<u>While</u> we were dancing…*

15.8. Don't use *things* as a generic substitute for a more precise word.

No: *This includes things like electricity and water.*

Yes: *This includes services like electricity and water.*

15.9. Don't use *said* as an adjective in reference to something mentioned in a preceding sentence.

No: *Holding the diamond necklace tightly, she snuck into the room and closed the door. She placed said necklace on the counter and…*

Yes: *Holding the diamond necklace tightly, she snuck into the room and closed the door. She placed it on the counter and…*

15.10. Don't end a clause or a sentence with *at all*.

No: *The book had no footnotes at all, so I wasn't sure what to make of it.*

Yes: *The book had no footnotes, so I wasn't sure what to make of it.*

No: *It never appeared in print at all.*

Yes: *It never appeared in print.*

15.11. Avoid the words *ironic* and *deconstruct/deconstruction* as well as the expressions *leading question* and *beg the question*. Almost everyone uses them incorrectly. It is especially egregious when someone assumes that *deconstruction* is a synonym for *destruction*.

15.12. Watch where you employ *only*. It often needs to be closer to the end of a sentence. Let's say you write the following:

He <u>only</u> goes grocery shopping on Sunday mornings.

This means he does nothing else on Sunday mornings, not even sleeping, and he might grocery shop on any other day from Monday to Saturday. If, in contrast, you write the following:

He goes grocery shopping <u>only</u> on Sunday mornings.

This means he grocery shops exclusively on Sundays while possibly doing other activities, such as clipping his toe nails. And he does no grocery shopping on any other day from Monday to Saturday.

15.13. Use the pronoun *one* consistently throughout a sentence.

No: *<u>One</u> is more likely to suffer a heart attack if <u>they</u> are obese.*

Yes: *<u>One</u> is more likely to suffer a heart attack if <u>one</u> is obese.*

Better still, avoid the pronoun *one*. It comes across as stuffy and tends to result in abstract sentences, leaving one without an image in one's head of the human beings represented by *one*. (See what I mean?) As a result, I recommend using the more informal *you* even in formal writing.

Better: *<u>You</u> are more likely to suffer a heart attack if <u>you</u> are obese.*

15.14. It's generally acceptable to use *data* in the singular (sing.), but purists will insist that *data*—a Latin word—should only be used in the plural (pl.) while *datum* should be used for the singular. If you want to please the purists, there is a way to ensure you use the plural correctly: In your mind, substitute *statistics* for *data*.

No: *The <u>statistics</u> <u>is</u> clear.*
Yes: *The <u>statistics</u> <u>are</u> clear.*
Yes: *The <u>data</u> <u>are</u> clear.*

Also note the difference between *criterion* (sing.) and *criteria* (pl.) as well as *phenomenon* (sing.) and *phenomena* (pl.)

15.15. Have *to* (not *and*) between *try* and a second verb that is in the infinitive.

No: *I will try and get it right.*
Yes: *I will try to get it right.*

The *and* usage occurs often in pop songs because, I assume, it's easier to sing *and* (with a silent "d") than *to* ("gonna try an' love again").

15.16. Avoid using *etc.*, *and so on*, or *and so forth* when it's not evident what might come next.

Yes: *The pattern was 2, 4, 6, 8, etc.*
Ok: *He packed shirts, pants, socks, and so on.*

This one is fine, as we can surmise what other items might be in his suitcase—likely underwear, sweaters, and a belt, but not a lampshade or a grandfather clock.

No: *They visited a museum, a nature preserve, an ice-cream parlour, and so forth.*

This is unclear. It's anyone's guess where they went after they quaffed down their ice cream.

15.17. Don't use *e.g.* (write out *for example*) or *i.e.* (write out *that is*). If a reader has to say the words in her head, you may as well spell them out for her.

15.18. Avoid clichés like the you-know-what. The following are some examples (among potentially thousands): *all walks of life, blissful ignorance, bring to the table, dead as a doornail, fall on deaf ears, grind to a halt, icing on the cake, marked contrast, peas in a* *pod, rock the boat, sitting duck, storm of protest, think outside the box.*

15.19. Avoid hackneyed business terms. A list of these atrocities includes *actionable, bottom line, deliverables, ideate, impactful, incentivize, learnings, pressurize, proactive, rightsize, synergize, takeaway,* and the oxymoronic *negative growth.*

15.20. Delete "throat clearing" phrases. These appear at the beginning of a sentence, usually concluding with *that.* Just say what you have to say.

The fact that…
It should be noted that…
It is interesting that…
It is important to add that…

15.21. The emphatic form of the verb *do* is often unnecessary.

No: *I do have some candy.*
Yes: *I have some candy.*

The emphatic form of *do* works better in conversation than in writing.

15.22. The emphatic intensive pronoun is often unnecessary.

No: *I myself have not seen the film.*
Yes: *I have not seen the film.*

15.23. Never use *former… latter.* Never ever. It requires the reader to look back at a previous sentence to see who's who (or what's what). Typically, the best solution is to default to two sentences; that is, don't try to cram everything into a single, winding sentence. The following is from *Jacobin*, a political magazine:

WRITING DOS AND DON'TS 151

Actual: *While Hofstader deserves credit for jump-starting the serious study of conspiracy theories and theorists, his scholarship linked the <u>former</u> to a pseudo-psychological diagnosis and positioned the <u>latter</u> as irrational, alienated individuals on the fringes of both society and politics.*

Revised: *Hofstader deserves credit for jump-starting the serious study of conspiracies. But his scholarship linked conspiracy theories to a pseudo-psychological diagnosis, while positioning the theorists themselves as irrational, alienated individuals on the fringes of both society and politics.*

15.24. It is especially irritating when writers use a *latter* without a *former*. The following is a made-up example based on a passage in a book on capitalism.

No: *We find in capitalist societies many struggles over race, gender, colonialism, climate change, labour processes, militarism, and <u>democracy</u>. It is now becoming clearer than ever that the <u>latter</u> appears intimately related to…*

This is a version of "elegant variation," where the author wants to forego repeating a word but then causes confusion by doing so. In this example, I suspect most people reading *latter* would have to glance back to see what it refers to. These readers could have avoided any resulting neck strain if the author had just re-employed *democracy* ("It is now becoming clearer than ever that *democracy* appears…"). This also would have enabled the author to delete that cumbersome, and rather lonely, *latter*.

15.25. Don't use *respectively* to avoid repeating a word or two. Like *former… latter*, it will have readers scurrying backward in order to understand your point.

No: *The cat's and the dog's <u>share</u> of the pet food budget was 40 per cent and 60 per cent <u>respectively</u>.*

Yes: *The cat's <u>share</u> of the pet food budget was 40 per cent; the dog's <u>share</u> was 60 per cent.*

15.26. Phrase your thoughts in positive terms. Especially when you use more than one negative in a sentence—and much like *former... latter* and *respectively*—you force readers to pause to figure out what you mean.

No: *This definition is <u>not unproblematic</u>.*
Yes: *This definition is <u>problematic</u>.*

No: *They are <u>not dissimilar</u>.*
Yes: *They are <u>similar</u>.*

Multiple negatives can sometimes make it almost impossible to understand what a writer is saying. The following is an example from a statement by a publisher's imprint:

Actual: *The Salvage Collective <u>does not believe</u>, put simply, that radical writing <u>should not</u> also strive for beauty.*
Revised: *The Salvage Collective <u>believes</u>, put simply, that radical writing <u>should</u> also strive for beauty.*

Now, isn't that not more unbeautiful?

15.27. Don't use an expression like "at the turn of the twentieth century."

No: *The philosophy garnered more advocates <u>at the turn of the twentieth century</u>.*
Yes: *The philosophy garnered more advocates <u>in the early twentieth century</u>.*
Better: *The philosophy garnered more advocates <u>in the early 1900s</u>.*
Best: *The philosophy garnered more advocates <u>between 1900 and 1914</u>.*

15.28. Don't put more essential information after less essential information (which you incorrectly designated as less essential because you placed it between commas).

No: *The owner of the bookstore on Main Street, <u>Mary Ozick</u>, died last night.*

Yes: *<u>Mary Ozick</u>, the owner of the bookstore on Main Street, died last night.*

Note, too, that deciding what information is more essential is not always cut and dry.

15.29. A pronoun needs to refer unambiguously to its antecedent, a previously mentioned noun it is meant to stand in for.

<u>Tom</u> watched as <u>his</u> cat <u>Gilbert</u> ate dinner, then <u>he</u> turned on <u>his</u> laptop to see how the game was going.

The first *his* clearly refers to Tom, but the *he* and the second *his* seem to refer to Gilbert, who we now assume is the proud owner of a password and opposable thumbs. Be especially careful when you use the pronouns *it* or *this*, which tend to become unmoored from their antecedents.

15.30. Do not use a feminine pronoun to refer to a ship (unless you are a sailor), a country (unless you are a historian who is more than one hundred years old), or nature (no exceptions permitted).

No: *The* Titanic *and many of <u>her</u> crew and passengers...*
Yes: *The* Titanic *and many of <u>its</u> crew and passengers...*

No: *Greece and <u>her</u> people are...*
Yes: *Greece and <u>its</u> people are...*

No: *Nature showed <u>her</u> power last night...*
Yes: *Nature showed <u>its</u> power last night...*

15.31. Numbers or adjectives like *many* imply separation or difference. You don't need to tell us so.

No: *There are six <u>separate</u> investigations.*
Yes: *There are six investigations.*

No: *There are nine <u>assorted</u> flavours.*
Yes: *There are nine flavours.*

No: *She speaks three <u>different</u> languages.*
Yes: *She speaks three languages.*

No: *The chickens ran in many <u>various</u> directions.*
Yes: *The chickens ran in many directions.*

15.32. In most instances, you should be able to change large numbers, or numbers with plenty of decimals, to something that is easier on the eyes. If so, you don't need to adorn the number with words like *roughly*, *approximately*, or *almost*, since every reader except the thickest dullard should understand that the number has been rounded.

No: *It had a combined worth of <u>$2.875 billion</u>.*
Yes: *It had a combined worth of <u>$2.9 billion</u>.*

No: *Between 1989 and 2014, their wages rose <u>13.96 per cent</u>.*
Yes: *Between 1989 and 2014, their wages rose <u>14 per cent</u>.*

There will be times when precision is important to maintain.

Within a few hours, her temperature had risen from 36.5 degrees to 38.1.

He ran the hundred-yard dash in 9.87 seconds.

15.33. Don't use more words that you have to.

No: *more and more*	**Yes:** *more*	**Or:** *increasingly*
No: *less and less*	**Yes:** *less*	**Or:** *decreasingly*
No: *further and further*	**Yes:** *further*	
No: *whether or not*	**Yes:** *whether*	
No: *sit down*	**Yes:** *sit*	
No: *price point*	**Yes:** *price*	

15.34. Don't add one or more useless words to the discussion.

No: *completely destroyed*	**Yes:** *destroyed*
No: *completely surrounded*	**Yes:** *surrounded*
No: *total annihilation*	**Yes:** *annihilation*
No: *join together*	**Yes:** *join*
No: *end result*	**Yes:** *result*
No: *close scrutiny*	**Yes:** *scrutiny*
No: *unfilled vacancy*	**Yes:** *vacancy*
No: *ten in number*	**Yes:** *ten*
No: *blue in colour*	**Yes:** *blue*
No: *large in size*	**Yes:** *large*

15.35. Don't use two words (connected by *and*) that have identical meanings. Pick (or choose!) one from the following pairs and run with it.

cease and desist
first and foremost
null and void
peace and quiet
pick and choose

15.36. Always try to replace wordy phrases with a precise word.

due to the fact that = *because*
as a consequence of = *because*
for the purpose of = *to*
in order to = *to*
on the condition that = *if*
in the event that = *if*
with the exception of = *except*
until such time as = *until*
in the vicinity of = *near*

15.37. Delete unnecessary prepositions.

No: *It fell off of the desk.*
Yes: *It fell off the desk.*

No: *I'm going in to the church.*
Yes: *I'm going in the church.*

No: *I called up an old friend.*
Yes: *I called an old friend.*

15.38. Either option in the following pairs is acceptable, but choose *among* over *amongst*, *backward* over *backwards*, *exploitive* over *exploitative*, *preventive* over *preventative*, *toward* over *towards*, and *use* over *utilize*. If you want to know why, just read the words out loud.

15.39. It is important to expand your vocabulary, but it's best to ignore words with multiple syllables that are difficult to pronounce, words we almost never use when speaking. The reader's tongue almost always trips over these obstacles. Some of my least favourites—surely among the ugliest words in the language—include *concatenation, desuetude, eschew, execrable, ignominious, indefatigable, ineluctable, quotidian, verisimilitude, vicissitudes,* and *vituperative.*

When I see one of these freaks, the vein in my neck starts to vibrate. There is no need for writers to jump up and down, waving their arms in the air like four-year-olds trying to attract attention to themselves. Readers should be drawn to your words because of their plain beauty, not their showiness. This also has the virtue of keeping your readers in a state of balance, partly alert and partly relaxed. We know that, more than most, academics tend to be on their guard, gripping their pencils tightly, ready to pounce like a pride of lions on a slower-than-average wildebeest. But even these folks should, much of the time, experience a trancelike sensation in their mind when reading, the same pleasurable feeling the body has when it floats on water. It's your job to create that feeling.

That means, in this instance, replacing the freaks noted above with words like *linking, disuse, avoid, bad, embarrassing, unstoppable, unavoidable, daily, appears real, change of fortune,* and *abusive (language).* Persnickety writers will say, "Those are not exact synonyms." Grateful readers will reply, "We don't care."

PART IV. *The End*

APPENDIX 1
NONFICTION BOOKS TO INSPIRE YOUR WRITING

I mentioned earlier that the best way to become a first-rate writer is to be an incessant and voracious reader, someone who always has a book on the go. The following is a list of over one hundred nonfiction books, most of which have been published in the last decade. You should be able to find at least a dozen or so that strike you as interesting (you can take them for a test drive on Google Books). If you are not yet much of a reader, they can help you get in the habit. If you already are one, you now have additional titles to add to your got-to-get-to pile.

Happy reading!

Note that if you conduct a search for these books, the bibliographic information you find may differ from what is noted here, depending on whether the books were published in the United States, the United Kingdom, or Canada, and whether they are hardbacks or paperbacks.

Abdurraqib, Hanif. *A Little Devil in America: Notes in Praise of Black Performance*. Random House, 2021.

Aciman, André. *Homo Irrealis: Essays*. Farrar, Straus and Giroux, 2021.

Alexie, Sherman. *You Don't Have to Say You Love Me: A Memoir*. Back Bay Books, 2019.

Allende, Isabel. *The Soul of a Woman: On Impatient Love, Long Life, and Good Witches*. Translated by Isabel Allende. Ballantine, 2021.

Anderson, Darren. *Inventory: A Memoir*. Farrar, Straus and Giroux, 2020.

Applebaum, Anne. *Twilight of Democracy: The Seductive Lure of Authoritarianism*. Signal, 2021.

Armitage, Simon. *Walking Away: A Poet's Journey*. Liveright, 2013.

Bakewell, Sarah. *At the Existentialist Café: Freedom, Being, and Apricot Cocktails*. Knopf Canada, 2016.

Beard, Jo Ann. *Festival Days*. Little, Brown, 2021.

Beard, Mary. *SPQR: A History of Ancient Rome*. Liveright, 2016.

Bevins, Vincent. *If We Burn: The Mass Protest Decade and the Missing Revolution*. Public Affairs, 2023.

Boyer, Anne. *The Undying: Pain, Vulnerability, Mortality, Medicine, Art, Time, Dreams, Data, Exhaustion, Cancer, and Care*. Farrar, Straus and Giroux, 2019.

Broom, Sarah M. *The Yellow House: A Memoir*. Grove, 2019.

Brum, Eliane. *Banzeiro Òkòtó: The Amazon as the Center of the World*. Translated by Diane Whitty. Graywolf, 2023.

Bryson, Bill. *The Body: A Guide for Occupants*. Anchor Canada, 2021.

Caldwell, Gail. *Bright Precious Thing: A Memoir*. Random House, 2020.

Carrère, Emmanuel. *Yoga*. Translated by John Lambert. Farrar, Straus and Giroux, 2022.

Carson, Anne. *Wrong Norma*. New Directions, 2024.

Coates, Ta-Nehisi. *We Were Eight Years in Power: An American Tragedy*. One World, 2018.

Cusk, Rachel. *Coventry: Essays*. Farrar, Straus and Giroux, 2019.
Davis, Lydia. *Essays One*. Farrar, Straus and Giroux, 2019.
Didion, Joan. *Blue Nights*. Vintage, 2012.
Diski, Jenny. *Why Didn't You Just Do What You Were Told? Essays*. Bloomsbury, 2020.
Dyer, Geoff. *The Last Days of Roger Federer: And Other Endings*. Canongate, 2022.
Ernaux, Annie. *A Girl's Story*. Translated by Alison L. Strayer. Seven Stories Press, 2020.
Fadiman, Anne. *The Wine Lover's Daughter: A Memoir*. Farrar, Straus and Giroux, 2018.
Febos, Melissa. *Girlhood: Essays*. Illustrations by Forsyth Harmon. Bloomsbury, 2022.
Filkins, Dexter. *The Forever War*. Vintage, 2009.
Forché, Carolyn. *What You Have Heard Is True: A Memoir of Witness and Resistance*. Penguin, 2019.
Frank, Thomas. *The People, No: A Brief History of Anti-Populism*. Metropolitan, 2020.
Franzen, Jonathan. *The End of the End of the Earth: Essays*. Farrar, Straus and Giroux, 2018.
Gay, Roxane. *Hunger: A Memoir of (My) Body*. Harper Perennial, 2018.
Gessen, Masha. *Surviving Autocracy*. Riverhead, 2020.
Gornick, Vivian. *The Odd Woman and the City: A Memoir*. Farrar, Straus and Giroux, 2016.
Handke, Peter. *Quiet Places: Collected Essays*. Translated by Krishna Winston and Ralph Manheim. Farrar, Straus and Giroux, 2022.
Hedges, Chris. *America: The Farewell Tour*. Simon and Schuster, 2018.
Hemon, Aleksandar. *My Parents: An Introduction / This Does Not Belong to You*. MCD Books, 2019.
Highway, Tomson. *Laughing with the Trickster: On Sex, Death, and Accordions*. House of Anansi Press, 2022.

Hochschild, Adam. *Lessons from a Dark Time: And Other Essays.* University of California Press, 2018.

Isenberg, Nancy. *White Trash: The 400-Year Untold History of Class in America.* Penguin, 2017.

Jamie, Kathleen, *Surfacing.* Penguin, 2019.

Jefferson, Margo. *Constructing a Nervous System: A Memoir.* Granta, 2022.

Jerkins, Morgan. *This Will Be My Undoing: Living at the Intersection of Black, Female, and Feminist in (White) America.* Harper Perennial, 2018.

Johnson, Lacy M. *The Reckonings: Essays on Justice for the Twenty-First Century.* Scribner, 2019.

Keefe, Patrick Radden. *Empire of Pain: The Secret History of the Sackler Dynasty.* Bond Street Books, 2021.

King, Charles. *Gods of the Upper Air: How a Circle of Renegade Anthropologists Reinvented Race, Sex, and Gender in the Twentieth Century.* Anchor, 2020.

Kisner, Jordan. *Thin Places: Essays from In Between.* Picador, 2021.

Klay, Phil. *Uncertain Ground: Citizenship in an Age of Endless, Invisible War.* Penguin, 2022.

Klein, Naomi. *Doppelganger: A Trip into the Mirror World.* Farrar, Straus and Giroux, 2023.

Kolbert, Elizabeth. *The Sixth Extinction: An Unnatural History.* Henry Holt, 2014.

Kureishi, Hanif. *What Happened? Stories and Essays.* Faber and Faber, 2019.

Kushner, Rachel. *The Hard Crowd: Essays, 2000–2020.* Scribner, 2021.

Laing, Olivia. *Everybody: A Book About Freedom.* Norton, 2021.

Lockwood, Patricia. *Priestdaddy.* Riverhead, 2018.

Lopez, Barry. *Embrace Fearlessly the Burning World: Essays.* Random House, 2022.

Macdonald, Helen. *H Is for Hawk.* Grove, 2016.

Macfarlane, Robert. *Underland: A Deep Time Journey.* Penguin, 2020.

Malcolm, Janet. *Still Pictures: On Photography and Memory.* Farrar, Straus and Giroux, 2023.

Mann, Sally. *Hold Still: A Memoir with Photographs.* Back Bay Books, 2016.

Mantel, Hilary. *A Memoir of My Former Self: A Life in Writing.* Edited by Nicholas Pearson. Henry Holt, 2023.

Marías, Javier. *Between Eternities: And Other Writings.* Edited by Alexis Grohmann. Translated by Margaret Jull Costa. Vintage International, 2018.

McMillan Cottom, Tressie. *Thick: And Other Essays.* New Press, 2019.

McPhee, John. *The Patch.* Picador, 2019.

Miles, Tiya. *All That She Carried: The Journey of Ashley's Sack, a Black Family Keepsake.* Random House, 2022.

Morrison, Toni. *The Source of Self-Regard: Selected Essays, Speeches, and Meditations.* Vintage International, 2020. Also published as *Mouth Full of Blood.*

Nelson, Maggie. *On Freedom: Four Songs of Care and Constraint.* McClelland and Stewart, 2021.

Nicolson, Adam. *How to Be: Life Lessons from the Early Greeks.* Farrar, Straus and Giroux, 2023.

O'Brien, Edna. *Country Girl: A Memoir.* Back Bay Books, 2014.

Orlean, Susan. *The Library Book.* Simon and Schuster, 2018.

Pamuk, Orhan. *Istanbul: Memories and the City.* Translated by Maureen Freely. Knopf, 2007.

Patchett, Ann. *These Precious Days: Essays.* HarperCollins, 2021.

Penman, Ian. *It Gets Me Home, This Curving Track: Objects and Essays, 2012–2018.* Fitzcarraldo Editions, 2019.

Raban, Jonathan. *Father and Son: A Memoir.* Knopf, 2023.

Rankine, Claudia. *Just Us: An American Conversation.* Graywolf, 2020.

Roy, Arundhati. *My Seditious Heart: Collected Nonfiction.* Haymarket, 2019.

Rundell, Katherine. *Super-Infinite: The Transformations of John Donne.* Picador, 2023.

Rush, Elizabeth. *Rising: Dispatches from the New American Shore*. Milkweed, 2019.

Rushdie, Salman. *Knife: Meditations After an Attempted Murder*. Knopf Canada, 2024.

Russo, Richard. *The Destiny Thief: Essays on Writing, Writers, and Life*. Vintage, 2019.

Sedaris, David. *The Best of Me*. Little, Brown, 2020.

Shteyngart, Gary. *Little Failure: A Memoir*. Random House, 2014.

Simic, Charles. *The Life of Images: Selected Prose*. Ecco, 2017.

Sischy, Ingrid. *Nothing Is Lost: Selected Essays of Ingrid Sischy*. Edited by Sandra Brant. Knopf, 2018.

Smith, Patti. *Year of the Monkey*. Vintage Canada, 2020.

Smith, Zadie. *Feel Free: Essays*. Penguin, 2018.

Solnit, Rebecca. *Recollections of My Nonexistence*. Penguin, 2021.

Stepanova, Maria. *In Memory of Memory: A Romance*. Translated by Sasha Dugdale. Book*hug Press, 2021.

Tan, Amy. *Where the Past Begins: A Writer's Memoir*. HarperCollins, 2017.

Thrall, Nathan. *A Day in the Life of Abed Salama: Anatomy of a Jerusalem Tragedy*. Metropolitan, 2023.

Thurman, Judith. *A Left-Handed Woman: Essays*. Farrar, Straus and Giroux, 2022.

Tolentino, Jia. *Trick Mirror: Reflections on Self-Delusion*. Random House, 2019.

Traister, Rebecca. *Good and Mad: The Revolutionary Power of Women's Anger*. Simon and Schuster, 2019.

Trethewey, Natasha. *Memorial Drive: A Daughter's Memoir*. Ecco, 2020.

Vaillant, John. *Fire Weather: The Making of a Beast*. Knopf Canada, 2023.

Wade, Francesca. *Square Haunting: Five Writers in London Between the Wars*. Crown, 2021.

Wagamese, Richard. *Embers: One Ojibway's Meditations*. Douglas and McIntyre, 2016.

Walker, Alice. *The Cushion in the Road: Meditation and Wandering as the Whole World Awakens to Being in Harm's Way.* New Press, 2014.

Wallace, David Foster. *Both Flesh and Not: Essays.* Back Bay Books, 2013.

Wallace-Wells, David. *The Uninhabitable Earth: Life After Warming.* Tim Duggan Books, 2020.

Ward, Jesmyn. *Men We Reaped: A Memoir.* Bloomsbury, 2014.

Westover, Tara. *Educated: A Memoir.* Random House, 2018.

Whitehead, Colson. *The Noble Hustle: Poker, Beef Jerky, and Death.* Anchor, 2015.

Wilkerson, Isabel. *Caste: The Origins of Our Discontents.* Random House, 2020.

Williams, Terry Tempest. *Erosion: Essays of Undoing.* Sara Crichton Books, 2019.

Willis, Ellen. *The Essential Ellen Willis.* Edited by Nona Willis Aronowitz. University of Minnesota Press, 2014.

Wood, James. *Serious Noticing: Selected Essays, 1997–2019.* Picador, 2021.

Woolf, Virginia. *A Room of One's Own / Three Guineas.* Edited by Michèle Barrett. Penguin, 2000. First published 1929, 1938.

Zauner, Michelle. *Crying in H Mart: A Memoir.* Knopf, 2021.

APPENDIX 2
SOME ADVICE FOR INSTRUCTORS

Research papers are dreaded by students and often by instructors as well, who must mark and grade them. Writing a research paper is like a half-marathon for the brain. I know this is true even for many faculty members who have PhDs. Some trip on the hurdle of conceptualizing a project. Others get anxious over writing, either unable to start or unable to finish. Finding the time to write is also a challenge, so some give up putting pen to paper during the academic year, thinking if they have large blocks of time, perhaps next summer or during a sabbatical, then all will go smoothly. But it never does. Many academics, then, struggle to express themselves when they attempt to articulate their research findings. You don't have to look far to witness this struggle. Read the abstract of almost any journal article and you will see at play the battle between an author's thoughts and the words that made it onto the page, words that were probably revised dozens of times.

Given this, instructors should not be harsh on their students—especially first- and second-year students—all of whom are, in some ways, apprentice academics, just starting to acquire their trade. Instructors should begin from the premise that students can write. They just can't write complex research papers the moment they step foot on campus. This is something they will learn to do, with your help, with varying degrees of success, over the course of four or more years.

The key is *with your help*. I taught and conducted research in an interdisciplinary program (Social Welfare and Social Development). I designed dozens of assignments for my students and marked and graded thousands of them. I learned quickly, thanks to the work of John C. Bean, that clear assignment questions are critical for enabling students to produce papers ranging from competent to exceptional. This means designing writing tasks that are rooted in *controversy*. You frame a question that makes it feasible for students to formulate a single response from a number of eminently reasonable responses.

In order to do this well, your assignment instructions should not have more than one question, the one you need to have answered. So, don't string together four or five questions, where all of them seem to be of equal importance. If you do this, you guarantee that your students will be unable to write focused arguments, and you will have to trudge through dozens of badly organized papers, for which you will have to claim some responsibility. (Note that it's fine to have some background information that ends with the single question you expect students to answer.)

You also need to think about how you will respond to the papers you receive. Almost all students will ignore any detailed comments you make on the use of grammar and punctuation (though you can give them general advice such as, "you frequently misuse semicolons"). As a result, don't obsess over the many "micro" errors you will surely discover. Don't edit your students' papers. That is, don't take on the role of a line editor, agonizing over sentence structure, word choice, verb tense, and the like. This wastes your time, and it will not help them to improve their work. Perhaps mark up one page, or one paragraph, to give the student an idea of the types of mistakes they make, and let them know you marked only this small portion, so they don't assume the rest of the paper is flawless.

Overall, the comments you make should address "macro" issues, such as, for instance, research, evidence, paragraph structure, and the flow of the argument, and you can do so by employing the numeric codes in this book, to provide students with rapid feedback in the margins of their papers. Give most of your attention to the quality of the student's thesis and how well they carried it out. So, when you are grading, read only for ideas and evidence—as you would with a colleague's draft paper—and try to gloss over the inevitable mistakes you'll see here and there in grammar and style. As you are reading, if you focus exclusively on the argument, you will discover, perhaps to your surprise, that your students are much more intelligent than you give them credit for.

After you have completed marking, you must, of course, assign a grade. I struggled for many years on how to do this effectively. Over a long process of trial and error, I developed the following rubric:

CATEGORY	MAXIMUM GRADE	YOUR GRADE
Context	5	
Thesis	10	
Road Map	5	
Conclusion	10	
Quotations	10	
Paragraphs	10	
Writing	10	
Argument	20	
Research	20	

GRADE: _____

I gave 20 points for research and 20 points for the quality of the argument. This sent the message that what I most valued was their ability to read a number of sources and develop a powerful case backed by substantial evidence. I awarded 20 points for the introduction: 10 for the thesis and 5 each for the context and road map. This emphasized that the first three paragraphs had to be tended to, because if done well, they make it possible for the student to flourish in the rest of the paper. I also gave 10 points each for the conclusion, the use of quotations, paragraphs, and general writing ability (mostly at the sentence level).

This rubric will enable you to provide students with precise feedback on particular tasks, to show them where they did well or not so well. What sometimes happens is that a student realizes they have a solid writing style with generally well-organized paragraphs; however, major weaknesses in their research produced major weaknesses in their argument. Another upside of my rubric is that once I added the numbers, the student's grade almost always came within a single point of the one I would have given if I graded holistically.

FURTHER READING

Instructors can find plenty of great advice on how to structure assignments in John C. Bean and Dan Melzer's *Engaging Ideas*. I read the first edition of this book (with Bean as the sole author) early in my career, and it had a profound effect on my work.

BIBLIOGRAPHY

The American Heritage Desk Dictionary and Thesaurus. Houghton Mifflin Harcourt, 2014.

American Psychological Association. *Publication Manual of the American Psychological Association.* 7th ed. APA, 2020.

Barrett, Grant. *Perfect English Grammar: The Indispensable Guide to Excellent Writing and Speaking.* Zephyros Press, 2016.

Bean, John C., and Dan Melzer. *Engaging Ideas: The Professor's Guide to Integrating Writing, Critical Thinking, and Active Learning in the Classroom.* 3rd ed. Jossey-Bass, 2021.

Booth, Wayne C., Gregory G. Colomb, Joseph M. Williams, Joseph Bizup, and William T. FitzGerald. *The Craft of Research.* 5th ed. University of Chicago Press, 2024.

Bryson, Bill. *Bryson's Dictionary for Writers and Editors.* Broadway, 2008.

Bryson, Bill. *Bryson's Dictionary of Troublesome Words: A Writer's Guide to Getting It Right.* Anchor Canada, 2002.

Casagrande, June. *The Best Punctuation Book, Period: A Comprehensive Guide for Every Writer, Editor, Student, and Businessperson.* Ten Speed Press, 2014.

Casagrande, June. *It Was the Best of Sentences, It Was the Worst of Sentences: A Writer's Guide to Crafting Killer Sentences*. Ten Speed Press, 2010.

Dreyer, Benjamin. *Dreyer's English: An Utterly Correct Guide to Clarity and Style*. Random House, 2019.

Forsyth, Mark. *The Elements of Eloquence: Secrets of the Perfect Turn of Phrase*. Berkley Books, 2014.

Foster, Thomas C. *How to Read Nonfiction Like a Professor: A Smart, Irreverent Guide to Biography, History, Journalism, Blogs, and Everything in Between*. Harper Perennial, 2020.

Graff, Gerald, and Cathy Birkenstein. *"They Say / I Say": The Moves That Matter in Academic Writing*. 6th ed. Norton, 2024.

Haag, Pamela. *Revise: The Scholar-Writer's Essential Guide to Tweaking, Editing, and Perfecting Your Manuscript*. Yale University Press, 2021.

Hart, Jack. *Wordcraft: The Complete Guide to Clear, Powerful Writing*. 2nd ed. University of Chicago Press, 2021.

Harvey, Gordon. *Writing with Sources: A Guide for Students*. 3rd ed. Hackett, 2017.

Landon, Brooks. *Building Great Sentences: How to Write the Kinds of Sentences You Love to Read*. Plume, 2013.

Lukeman, Noah. *The Art of Punctuation*. Oxford University Press, 2006. Also published as *A Dash of Style: The Art and Mastery of Punctuation*. Norton, 2006.

Modern Language Association of America. *MLA Handbook*. 9th ed. MLA, 2021.

The New American Roget's College Thesaurus in Dictionary Form. 3rd ed. Edited by Philip D. Morehead. Signet, 2002.

O'Conner, Patricia T. *Woe Is I: The Grammarphobe's Guide to Better English in Plain English*. 4th ed. Riverhead, 2019.

Paperback Oxford English Dictionary. 7th ed. Edited by Maurice Waite. Oxford University Press, 2012.

Patriquin, Larry. "How to Complete a Doctoral Dissertation in This Lifetime: Some Marbles of Wisdom." In *The Next Step* in *Studying Religion: A Graduate's Guide*, edited by Mathieu Courville. Continuum, 2007.

Pears, Richard, and Graham Shields. *Cite Them Right: The Essential Referencing Guide*. 12th ed. Bloomsbury Academic, 2022.

Ross-Larson, Bruce. *Edit Yourself: A Manual for Everyone Who Works with Words*. 2nd ed. Norton, 1996.

Ross-Larson, Bruce. *Powerful Paragraphs*. Norton, 1999.

Royal, Brandon. *The Little Red Writing Book: 20 Powerful Principles of Structure, Style, and Readability*. Writer's Digest Books, 2004.

Strunk, William, Jr., and E. B. White. *The Elements of Style*. 4th ed. Pearson Education, 2000.

Sword, Helen. *Stylish Academic Writing*. Harvard University Press, 2012.

Sword, Helen. *The Writer's Diet: A Guide to Fit Prose*. University of Chicago Press, 2016.

Taylor, Gordon. *A Student's Writing Guide: How to Plan and Write Successful Essays*. Cambridge University Press, 2009.

Truss, Lynne. *Eats, Shoots, and Leaves: The Zero Tolerance Approach to Punctuation*. Gotham, 2004.

University of Chicago Press. *The Chicago Manual of Style*. 18th ed. University of Chicago Press, 2024.

Weston, Anthony. *A Rulebook for Arguments*. 5th ed. Hackett, 2017.

Williams, Joseph M. *Style: Lessons in Clarity and Grace*. 9th ed. Pearson Education, 2007.

Wydick, Richard C. "Plain English for Lawyers." *California Law Review* 66, no. 4 (1978): 727–65.

ABOUT THE AUTHOR

Larry Patriquin earned a PhD in social and political thought at York University, Toronto in 1996. He was a faculty member at Nipissing University, North Bay, Ontario, from 1998 to 2023, teaching courses in social and economic justice, the history of social welfare, globalization, poverty, and work.

He is the author of *Democracy and Social Rights: A Path Toward Equality?* (Routledge, 2025), *Permanent Citizens' Assemblies: A New Model for Public Deliberation* (Rowman and Littlefield International, 2020), *Economic Equality and Direct Democracy in Ancient Athens* (Palgrave Macmillan, 2015), *Agrarian Capitalism and Poor Relief in England, 1500–1860: Rethinking the Origins of the Welfare State* (Palgrave Macmillan, 2007), and *Inventing Tax Rage: Misinformation in the* National Post (Fernwood, 2004). He is the editor of *The Ellen Meiksins Wood Reader* (Brill, 2012; Haymarket, 2013).

Bluesky: @larrypatriquin.bsky.social
ResearchGate: researchgate.net/profile/Larry-Patriquin
Web: larrypatriquin.com

www.ingramcontent.com/pod-product-compliance
Lightning Source LLC
Chambersburg PA
CBHW070150100426
42743CB00013B/2873